CONCEPT AND MEASUREMENT OF POVERTY

Concept and Measurement of Poverty

AROON SHARMA

ANMOL PUBLICATIONS
NEW DELHI (INDIA)

First Edition 1990

ISBN 81-7041-287-0

Published by :
ANMOL PUBLICATIONS
4378/4B, Gali Murari Lal,
Ansari Road, Daryaganj,
NEW DELHI-110002
Phone 3261597

Printed at :
Sangita Printers
Maujpur, DELHI-53.

Dedicated to the Memory of my dear Father
Prof. B.D. Sharma, whose moving spirit
enlivens and illuninates perennially
the inner recesses of my mind.

Preface

Concern for poverty in India has always been universal but after colonial rules, interest in poverty got momentum at first slowly and then by leaps and bounds. This was due to the realisation that there was nothing divine about poverty, that it was man made, that it was the outcome of retarded development of the forces of production within the limitation of archaic and stagnant relations of production and inadequately rewarded efforts, that it was the symptom of structural crises of present day socio-economic formation and that it could be remedied. This realization acted like a catalyst and fused the aspirations of masses (poor and non-poor) into a definite programme of actions against poverty.

During the early phase of the process of socio-economic transformation of Indian society, it was assumed that economic growth by itself will lead to the reduction in the incidence of poverty. However, around seventies it was felt that the benefits of growth have been shared inequitably and therefore, special efforts need to made to supplement the growth process by designing special programmes to cater to the need and development of identified groups. Formulation of programmes to mitigate poverty essentially required knowledge of what are now recognized as enormously complex causes. Empirical identification of these causes is a formidable task because of the conceptual issues involved in defining the many dimensions of poverty, the data constraints in measuring its incidence and the econometric problems in estimating the relationships between the causal factors and poverty levels. Despite enormous research, these problems have defied an universally accepted solution. Persistence of these problems inevitably suggest strengthening of efforts to evolve widely accepted framework of research on poverty and the present study is a modest effort in that direction.

The study is based on the thoughts expressed by large number of social scientists (Sociologists and Economists) in their innumerable writings and as such makes no claim to originality in any form. The main focus of the study is on the survey of ideas and opinions called from plethora of literature and arrange them in an appropriate manner consistent with the theme of study. The study is exploratory in nature and is designed into four chapters. The basic concepts of poverty are examined in chapter-I, while as the various techniques of measuring the degree of inequality and poverty are presented in chapter-II. These two chapters constitute the case of study and examine in detail the problems of conceptualisation and measurement of poverty. Chapter-III contains information on the incidence of poverty in India in its historical perspective and also reviews the various studies conducted in post-independence period to measure the extent of poverty in the country. Finally, the main observations and conclusions derived from the study are summed up in chapter-IV.

Acknowledgements

The present work would not have materialised without the guidance which I have received from my teacher Professor O.P. Kotwal, it is he who assiduously chiselled my raw mind and trained and equiped me with the logic and techniques to rationalise the stray ideas. I owe him a deep sense of gratitude for constructive criticism, valuable suggestions and continuous encouragement to accomplish this arduous work. My thanks are also due to Prof. Amarjeet Singh and Dr. O.P. Sharma for providing me helpful comments which have contributed to an improvement in the quality ot this work. I would like to express my gratitude to Dr. P.N. Abrol and Prof. Dhian Singh Bhau, who have helped me at all stages of production of this work.

AROON SHARMA

List of Tables

Contents

1

Concept of Poverty

Human race has lived for ages in a scarce economy. Co-existence of poverty and opulence both in time and space is the logical consequence of the operations of such an economy. Persistence and perpetuation of poverty was even considered necessary for maximum good of a minimum number of people. Thomas Mun upheld the view that "penury and want do make people wise and industrious". Arthur Young asserted that "every one but an idiot knows that the lower classes must be kept poor or they will never be industrious". John Law argued that "labourers were to blame for recurring high prices because of their 'insufferable habits of idleness contracted when food was cheap". David Hume also supported this belief by stating that in "years of scarcity, if it be hot extreme, the poor labour more and really live better than in years of great plenty when they indulge themselves in idleness and riot.[1] Poverty is also romanticized by suggesting that a poor who lives in the present develops a capacity for spontaneity, for the enjoyment of the sensual for the indulgence of impulse which is often blunted in the middle-class future-oriented person.

Another variant of the Doctrine of the Utility of the Poverty rests on the belief that there are sub-cultures in our society composed of people who prefer to be poor. Kenneth Boulding states that "a certain amount of the poverty of the hill billy or of the subsistence farmer and even perhaps of the urban slum dweller and of the buon, involves the rejection of the psychological cost of getting rich and a rejection of the middle-class way of life rather than the inability to find opportunities".

Carcenogenic consequences of poverty have emphasized that it is easier to praise poverty than to live in it. The doctrine of the Disutility of Poverty exhorts that social preferences based on human values are such that a reduction in poverty most certainly will enhance satisfactions. Poverty, thus, is socially undesirable and must therefore be bannished. Smolensky while stressing on the externality characteristic of poverty laid greater emphasis on the social consequences of poverty for the community than on the needs of the poor. He suggested that the "Poverty line should serve as an index of the disutility to the community of the persistence of Poverty".[3] In the same vein Rein expressed the view that people must not be allowed to become so poor that they offend or are hurtful to society. It is not so much the misery and plight of the poor but the discomfort and the cost of the community which is crucial to this view of poverty. We have a problem of poverty to the extent that the low income creates problems for those who are not poor. Poverty then consists of social problems correlated with low income. Hence only when income-conditioned problems are randomized can poverty be eliminated. To improve the level of living of the poor without reducing disutility to the rest of the community is insufficient".[4] Underlying theme in the writings of Titmus, considered poverty as more than the lack of income. He opined that "we cannot delineate the new frontiers of poverty unless we take account of the changing agents and characteristics of inequality".[5] Town send contended that the description, analysis and explanation of poverty in any country must proceed within the context of a general theory of stratification as applied to the social systems and sub-systems on a continuum ranging from the household or family at one extreme through local communities and national societies to world society at the other. Thus, according to him, "poverty must be regarded as a general form of relative deprivation which is the effect of maldistribution of resources viz., cash income, capital assets and three systems of benefits in kind-emyloyment benefits, public social service benefits and private benefits".[6]

These views relate the concept of poverty to the non-poor and do not consider poverty as a characteristic of the poor. Conceptualisation of poverty must highlight the problems confronting the poor (such as squalar disease, deprivation etc.) rather than its causes and consequences. It is thus contended that the concept of poverty must concern with the conditions of the poor.

Concept of Poverty

Two radically different approaches to the definition of poverty have been advanced; on the one hand, the 'Culture of poverty and on toe other, the Economic definition. The focus of cultural concept of poverty is on the internal attitudes and behaviour patterns of the poor with respect to the set of circumstances while as the economic concept highlights the external circumstances that condition a persons behaviour towards economic transactions.

(A) Culture of Poverty

One of the leading protagonists of this view, Oscar Lewis defines 'culture of poverty' as permanent way of life that develops among the poor people under the following set of conditions:

(1) a cash economy, wage labour and production for profit.

(2) a persistently high rate of unemployment and under-employment for unskilled labour.

(3) low wages.

(4) the failure to provide social political and economic organisation either on a voluntary basis or by government imposition, for the low income population.

(5) the existence of a bilateral kinship system rather than unilateral one and finally.

(6) the existence in the dominant class a set of values that stress the accumulation of wealth and property, the possibility of upward mobility and thrift and that explains low economic status as the result of personal inadequacy or inferiority.

Lewis described the culture of poverty in terms of some seventy inter-related social, economic and psychological traits. In the tradition of qualitative characterisation of poverty, Rossi and Blum have identified the following critical features of the poor.[8]

(1) *Labour-force Participation*: Long periods of unemployment. Public assistance is frequently a major source of income for extended periods.

(2) *Family and Interpersonnal Relations*: High rates of marital instability (desertion, diverse, separation), high incidence of housholds headed by females, high rates of illegitimacy, unstable and superficial interpersonal relationships characterised by considerable suspicion of persons outside the immediate household.

(3) *Community Characteristics*: Residential areas with very poorly developed voluntary associations and low levels of participation in such local voluntary associations exists.

(4) *Relationship to Large Society*: Little interest in or knowledge of the large society and its events; some degree of alientation from the larger society.

(5) *Value Orientations*: A sense of helpness and low sense of personnel efficacy, dogmatism and authoritarianism in political ideology, fundamentalist religious views with some strong inclinations towards belief in magical practices Low 'need achievement' and low levels of aspiration for the self.

Lewis held the view that the culture of poverty is not only sustained by external environment-povery—but also by internal systems of values and performances and interim personnel relationships that have a validity and life of their own and that are capable of persisting well after the externel circumstances have been modified or changed altogether. Poor people react to change in terms of prior values and behaviour patterns and adopt only those changes that are congrient with their culture. Poverty creates pathologies (adaptation to deprivation, degradation and destitution) that block the ability to adopt to non-pathological situations.[9] The culture of poverty is both an adaptation and a reaction of the poor to their marginal position in a class stratified, highly individuated capitalistic society. It represents an effort to cope with feelings of hopelessness and despair which develop from the realisation of the improbability of achieving success in terms of values and goals of the larger society. It is not only an adaptation to a set of objective conditions of the larger society but also tends to perpetuate itself from generation to generation. In fact intergenerational transmission of the characteristics of culture of poverty is near inevitability. At this point a question is begged, should the 'culture of poverty' refer only to those socio-cultural psychological traits and behaviour patterns of the poor that negate the upward movement or should it also include those persisting cultural patterns among the affluent that deliberately keep their fellow citizens poor. Viewed in this perspective, Lewis concept of 'Culture of poverty' is less concerned with culture than with situational factors that bring about culture, it is less a culture of poverty than a sociology of the underclass.[10] Basically, characteristics of the poor are situation rather than cultural "Poverty" writes Otis Dudley Duncan, "is not a trait but a condition".[11]

Conceptualisation of poverty along the cultural traits defies its measurement and therefore, whether or not culture of poverty is growing or shrinking remains unanswered. Similarly, whether or not the poor are better off or worse off than in past remains unexplained. Thus, the concept of poverty must be lucid and should reflect a single, definable, quantifiable characteristic that all poor families and only poor families possess.

(B) Definition of Poverty

Notwithstanding the probing of economists in the factors that account for poverty and their interest in poverty alleviation programmes, there is no integrated body of economic knowledge to get at the perfect understanding about poverty. Consequently, unlike economic stability and growth poverty for want of a theory is lost is economies.[12] Economists like Smith, Ricardo, Malthus, Mill, Marx, Marshall and Pigou have made occasional excursions into the area of poverty, but modern economists have not found poverty to their analytical taste. Discontentment with 'trickle down theory to help ameliorate poverty in a reasonable period and growing disutility of poverty to poor and non-poor have urged economists in recent years to chisel their tools and techniques to identify measure and eradicate poverty.

The central point of economic (objective) definition of poverty is that it is a property of the individuals situation rather than a characteristic of the individual or of his pattern of behaviour. Economists while agree that a meaningful concept of poverty should possess the attributes of measureability, objectivity, comparability and sensitivity to changes, yet they have not evolved an universally accepted concept of poverty depends on the approach adapted by the researcher to the phenomenon of poverty. Most of the research on poverty has adopted either of the following approaches to defining poverty.

1. Subsistance Approach

This approach to define poverty objectively refers to a condition of acute physical want-starvation, near starvation, or a diet-conducive to malnutrition and disease, lack of clothing or shelter necessary for protection from inclement elements, absence of minimal medical service. Poverty thus, is a situation which denies minimum food and shelter necessary to maintain/sustain life. Rountree perhaps was the first researcher to define poverty in subsistence terms. He opined:

"My primary poverty line represented the minimum sum on which physical efficiency could be maintained. It was a standard of bare subsistance rather than living. In calculating it the utmost economy was practised—Nothing must be bought but that which is absolutely necessary for the maintenance of physical health and what is bought must be the plainest and most economic description".[13]

It is thus possible to determine the norm of bare subsistence if human passions for frivolity are ruthlessly curbed. In the event of failure to regulate the spending behaviour of the consumer unit, it will move into a state of secondary poverty.[14] Secondary poverty exists when income is adequate to maintain a subsistence level, but the family fails to spend its income to purchase the necessities to sustain life and health. Gadgil states that "poverty is nothing but a standard of living below a certain minimum".[15] Following Rountree's work (1901) he distinguishes between two types of poverty:

(a) Primary poverty resulting from inadequate income, and

(b) Secondary poverty caused by an "ignorant and careless housekeeping and other improvident expenditure" of an adequate income.

In the same wake Martin Rein describes poverty as lack of the income needed to acquire the minimum necessities of life.[16] It is while true that starvation is the most telling aspect of poverty, but it should not be taken to mean actually dying of lack of food; rather badly fed and clothed, wretchedly housed and miserable in general.

Conceptualization of 'minimum necessities of life' in an objective manner confronts issues that are hard to resolve for the needs which are basic are conditioned not only by the physical and climatic environment but also by social structure and culture. Pre-requirement of minimum necessities' to sustain and procreate life also vary with age, sex, vocation and other attributes of the consuming unit therefore standardisation of a 'basket of necessities, needed to alleviate poverty is a difficult preposition. It is, thus, convenient to perceive that individuals with identical levels of income may, have different 'standards of living'. Similarly, families with different levels of income living in varying set of conditions/situations may not enjoy different 'standard of living.' Hence, the dividing line between the 'poor' and 'non-poor' is neither permanent nor uniform but changes both in space and time.

Notwithstanding these limitations, it is possible to lay a foundation for the economic definition of poverty with the help of the Neoclassical model of economic choice. According to this model every decision-making unit (individual/family) on the basis of his tastes, values and knowledge (assumed constant), has a 'system of preferences' among the given objects say necessities and luxuries. Given the system of preferences his 'choice' is constrained by the levels of income as is shown with the help of indifference curve analysis (Fig. I).

The model indicates that the consuming unit with preferences indicated by the indifference curves confronted with a budget limit and prices would choose to consume necessities at the rate R and luxuries at rate P. The model makes the distinction between preferences and constraints and limits the concept of poverty to the relatively objective constraint said of the problem. The ex-post facto choices reflect both preferences and constraints, but poverty is associated with

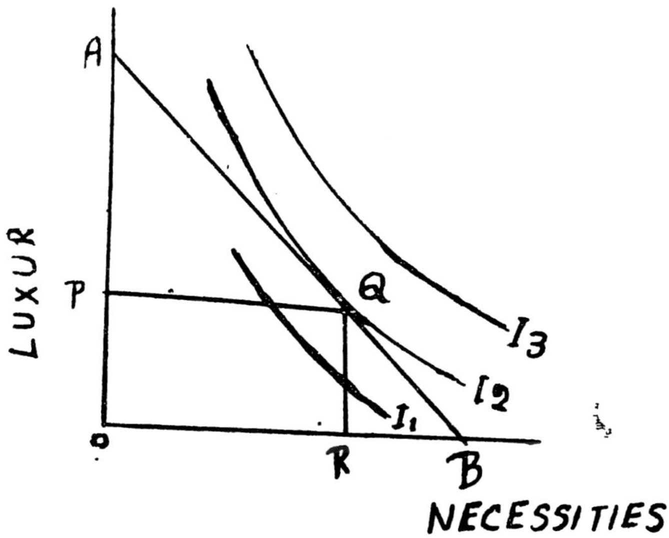

severe constriction of the choice imposed by the lower level of income. This definition of poverty is focussed on the mean for pursuit of betterment and argues that anyone with sufficient command over goods and services (income) will move to higher indifference curve and will be better off.

It must, however, be remembered that the external factors such as income and prices are subjected to variation. An increase in income would shift the constraint outward in a parallel manner and would lead to increased purchases of both commodities. A change in relative prices will rotate the constraints and thus, alter the level of purchases in such a manner that the consumption of good whose prices has increased will be reduced and that of the other will increase.

Constraint-oriented poverty concept is based on the theory of choice which require only ranking of alternatives. It is, thus, a useful concept for the purposes of comparing different situations before and after the changes in objective factors (income, prices) that determine the alternatives available to the consuming unit. This concept, however, is not helpful to measure the magnitude of poverty and therefore, is of little operational significance. Difficulties in the estimation of adequacy of non-food items comprising the basket of necessities has further minimised the significance of subsistence concept of poverty. Analysing the definition of poverty. Luck opined "The Wants to be considered here are the recognised biological necessities—food and drink. Little will be said about housing. The need for shelter varies according to locale and to social custom, it cannot be accurately measured. Fuel is essential for suvival in a cold environment, but this too is a regional and variable necessity. A similar consideration applies to clothing. The conventional biological definition of a necessity...excludes, except for reproduction, almost everything except food and water".[18] In the light of foregoing observations, it is perhaps reasonable to conclude that except food, their is an absence of standard of adequacy for essentials of living.

2. Nutritional Criteria of Defining Poerty

Another variant of biological concept of poverty is nutritional inadequacy. This definition implies a nutritional criterion of the minimum calorie intake below which there is undernutrition and also some 'norm' for determining the minimum cost of an adequate diet. The criteria of determining minimum nutritional requirements for calories and other essential nutrients does not itself have an unambiguous connotation in quantitative terms. Not only has it undergone change with time, but there has also been some dispute about using the average requirement, based on tht reference individual and equivalences for age and sex, as the criterion to be used for judging the nutritional status of an entire population".[19] Further, "even with food', Orshansky acknowledges, 'social conscience and custom dictate that there be not only sufficient quantity but sufficient variety to meet recommended nutritional goals and conform to customary eating patterns. Calories alone will not be enough. Yet food alone provides the best basis for measuring minimum requirements".[20] Orshansky goes on to advocate that the food plan should be developed on the "basis of an acceptable trade-off between nutritional standards and consumption patterns".[21]

There is, thus, a lack of agreement on the criteria of nutritional adequacy, for the the per capita requirement of calories depends upon such diverse factors age, sex, body weight occupation etc. of the consuming unit. The first and second Food and Agriculture Organisatiou (FAO) Committee on requirements suggested on energy expenditure per day of 3,200 calories for the reference man and 2,300 calories for the reference woman. There figures were reduced to 3,000 and 2,200 calories by the third FAO Committee in 1977.[22] Similarly, in case of India, the recommended calorie intake, first formulated in 1944, was revised in 1958 and then again in 1968 and in 1980 and is now placed at 2,400 calories for man and 1,900 calories for women per day.[23] The joint expert group of the FAO/WHO has recommended a minimum of 2,223 calories per capita per day for the people in Asia and Far East.[24] Dandekar and Rath have agreed for 2,250 calories as the irreducible minimum requirement or cut-off point.[25] Goven and Dixon have worked out the average energy requirement for thc Indian population at 1965 kilocalnries per day.[26] Planning Commission, Government of India recommends 2,400 calories per person per day for rural India and 2,100 calories for urban areas which works out to 2,350 calories for the population as a whole including both its urban and rural segments.[27] Acharya places the per capita requirement at 2,124 calories per day.[38] Sukhateme suggests the cut-off point for Indian population at 2,200 calories per head per day.[29] The research and Planning Division of ECAFE Secretariat assumes that for India, the minimum need for calorie intake is 2,500 plus 80 protein units.[30] Perusal of the studies on poverty conducted in India, indicates that most of them assume the calorie requirements at 2,250 per capita per day; which are to be obtained from the wide range of cereals, pulses fruits, vegetables, meat, eggs, milk etc.

It is apparent from the foregoing discussion that these two biological attributes of poverty (subsistence and nutritional) converge on the minimum food requirement' criteria, which in itself is faulty and defective problems associated with the subsistence concept of poverty are sought to be minimised by defining "necessities" as products on which the proportion of income expended declines as income rises "luxuries" as products on which expenditure rises, as income rises. Problems pertaining to the estimation of minimum requirement of 'non-food' items comprising the consumption basket are solved by converting expenditure for food into total expenditure with the help of following relationship :—

$$Te = FeE$$

where

Te=Cost of total consumption of the household

Fe=Expenditures for a minimum food basket

E=Size of Engels Co-officient[31]

Alternatively, expenditure on individual 'non-food' items is estimated with the help of the principal of "income elasticity of demand". For example, in case of clothing, as income of the family rises, it reaches a critical point where the number of additional units purchased declines and the price paid per units increases. This point is defined as the 'clothing poverty line'. Similarly, poverty lines or the cut-off points with respect to other items of the consumption basket are determined and then these points are pooled to draw the poverty line.

Nutritional criteria of poverty measurement is also subject to various limitations. There is no single 'subsistence' level which can be adopted for the estimation of the poverty line. There is no one level of food intake required for subsistence, but rather a broad range where physical efficiency declines with a falling intake of calories and proteins. Further, even if nutritional requirements are determined in terms of calories, proteins, etc., there would be problems arising from the disparity between expert judgement and actual consumption behaviour, not only due to the lack of dietary knowledge and uneconomic ways of expenditure by the poor families on food purchasing but also due to the eating habits which are profoundly influenced by culture and social traditions and conventions. In case of non-food items, there is even greater degree of arbitrariness, because minimum needs norms and the other factors change from region to region due to the climatic and social factors. Dantwala has also opined that a uniform 'norm' either in terms of the food basket which would provide minimum subsistence or its equivalent in money terms (due to price variations) would not be appropriate. Issues pertaining to the estimation of nutritional requirements with respect to the nature and degree of activity particularly the leisure activity have defined precise and flawless solutions.

Despite these shortcoming of the biological (nutritional aspect) concept of poverty, malnutrition constitute core of poverty. Attempts to dismiss this approach to define poverty are fraught with the possibility of adopting standards or criteria which do not highlight the central issue in the concept of poverty.

3. The Inequality Approach

This approach stresses that inequality and poverty are congruent and hence, co-terminus with each other. The bottom 10, 15 or more per cent of population on the income scale is poor and therefore, egalitarian distribution of income is both a necessary and sufficient condition for alleviation of poverty. Kuznet's generalisation based on International cross-section and time series evidence that income tends to be more unequally distributed in the developing (poor) economies than in those which have attained some degree of maturity[32] lends support to this approach. Earlier economists like Adam Smith, J.S. Mill and Alfred Marshall also recognised that the distribution of incomes affect poverty and observed that "although poverty was defined in absolute terms, each generation's 'poor' are mainly those significantly below the average income level".[33]

The stratificational approach necessitates the extension of the concept of poverty beyond the narrow limits of income and views the poor as those who are lagging behind relatively to others in society. Miller and Roby consider poverty and inequality as identical and support this contention by concluding:

> "In the spongy openness of the affluent society, poverty becomes not only a shorthand expression for inequality but a truncated phrase for the many ways in which the poor are different in society. Casting the issues of poverty in terms of stratification leads to regarding poverty as an issue of inequality. In this approach we move away from efforts to measure poverty lines with pseudo-scientific accuracy. Instead we look at the nature and size of the differences between the bottom 20 or 10 per cent and the rest of society. Our concern becomes one of narrowing the differences between those at the bottom and the better-off in each stratification dimension. In casting of the issues of poverty in terms of stratification, we do not wish to imply that the poor are a fixed homogenous group that shares a common outlook. Rather, we see the poor as those who lag behind the rest of society in terms of one or more dimensions of life—A stratificational approach implies that economic goals are not the only important objectives. The multi-dimensional concerns of stratification force attention to the non-economic aspects of inequality—The stratification perspective leads us to see that in dealing with poverty, we are dealing with the quality of life of individuals and not just their economic position. This means that not only individuals relationship to government but the quality of relationship to government but the quality of relationships among people in society are important".[34]

"Three broad concepts of poverty can be identified.

Poverty may be regarded as subsistence, inequality or externality. Subsistence is concerned with the minimum of provision needed to maintain health and working capacity. Its terms of reference are the capacity to survive and to maintain physical efficiency. Inequality is concerned with the relative position of income groups to each other. Poverty cannot be understood by isolating the poor and treating them as a special group. Society is seen as a series of stratified income layers and poverty is concerned with how the bottom layers fare relative to the rest of the society. Hence, the concept of poverty must be seen in the context of society as a whole. The study of the poor then depends on an understanding of the level of living of the rich, since it is these conditions relalive to each other that are critical in the conception of inequality. To understand the poor we must then study the affluent. Externality is concerned with the social consequences of poverty for the rest of society rather than in terms of the needs of the poor. The poverty line should serve 'as an index of the disutility to the community of the persistence of poverty".[35]

Bhatty (1974)[36] stated that both absolute and relative poverty are closely aligned to unequality in income distribution. Relative poverty arises entirely as a censequence of an unequal distribution of income irrespective of what the income level, or the corresponding state of deprivation, of the people at the bottom end of the income scale might be. Absolute poverty on the other hand expresses a collective view as deprivation in its some—what physical manifestation.

There is much to commend about this approach but to establish equivalence between inequality and poverty would be injudicious. Inequality and poverty although are not unrelated to each other, but they do not subsume each other. Re-distribution of income in favour of low income category must other things remaining the same, reduce inequality, but it may leave the perception of poverty unaltered. Similarly, a widespread reduction in the level of income may leave the pattern of income distribution and hence degree of inequality unchanged but will, most certainly cause intensification of poverty due to increase in hardship, misery and disease. Further, this approach is in appropriate for it ignores hunger and starvation, the two most important parameters of commonly understood concept of poverty. Thus, poverty is more than inequality, the poor undoubtedly receives an unequal share of resources, therefore, it must be related to the larger explanation of social inequality in general.

4 Relative Deprivation Approach

Deprivation is a multi-dimensional concept and connotes objectively evident conditions wherein people lack the basic elements to life and well-being. Since, unmet needs can be defined satisfactorily only in terms relative to the society in which they are found, therefore needs which are basic can be shown to be relative. Accordingly, Townsend suggests that "poverty must be regarded as a general form of relative deprivation which is the effect of the maldistribution of resources and that section of the population whose resources are so depressed from the mean as to be deprived of enjoying the benefits and participating in the activities which are customary in that society can be said to be in poverty. This not the same thing as saying that the poor are the 10 per cent or 20 per cent in every society with the least resources".[37] Townseed's concept of deprivation is much broader than the one represented on the score of per capita income or expenditure scale. He argues that, "possession by individual and families of relatively low resources does not automatically mean that they are in poverty, but only if they are thereby unable to have the types of diets, participate in activities and have the living conditions and amenities which are customary in that society".[38] Dorothy Wedderburn stated that "individuals, families and groups in the population can be said to be in poverty when they lack the resources to obtain the types of diets, participate in the activities and have the living conditions and amenities which are customary or/are at least widely encouraged or approved in the societies to which they belong. Their resources are so seriously below those commanded by the average individual or family that they are, in effect, excluded from ordinary living patterns, customs and activities".[39] Atkinson states that "a poverty line to separate deprivation from comforts is necessarily drawn in relation to social conventions and the customary living standards of a particular society and in this way somebody in the United States may be adjudged poor even though he has higher income than the average person in India".[40]

Thus, the concept of deprivation refers not only to the lack of resources whereby an average life style is denied to the individuals and families but also to the 'feeling' of deprivation for want of opportunities to catch up with the better privileged sections of society. Feeling of deprivation is also related to the expectations of individuals/families. It is argued that "conditions of deprivation" are of greater usage for it can be applied objectively to describe situations where people possess less of some desired attributes be it income, favourable employment or power, than do others".[41] Since, the choice regarding conditions of deprivation is conditioned by the individuals valuation (element of subjectivity, is involved) therefore 'feeling of deprivation cannot easily be dissociated from the conditions of deprivation. Thus, determination of 'conditions' objectively inevitably require 'concrete' understanding of feelings. In this context, Peter Townsend has aptly pointed out the importance of the "endeavour to define the style of living which is generally shared or approved in each society and find whether there is a point in the scale of distribution of resources below which families find it increasingly difficult to share in the customs, activities and diets comprising that style of living".[42] Further, feelings of deprivation are also influenced by the 'reference group' selected for comparison. This poses a grave problem for 'comparison' is not independent of community's political activity, information flow and changing perceptions of individuals which in turn affect an individuals expectations and his views about the fair share in the national cake and his right to share it, all this in turn influence the 'feeling of deprivation'. In this regard Dant Wala opined that "judging on the basis of U.S. official 'norm' for poverty in 1970, probably 99 per cent of India's population could be said to be living in poverty...therefore, frame of reference for identification and measurement of poverty has to be 'nation-rational".[43]

Concept of 'relative deprivation' is useful for the understanding of poverty as a socio-economic and non-political phenomenon but it cannot form the basis of conceptualisation of poverty for, absolute deprivation (starvation, malnutrition hardship etc. etc.) constitutes the central idea of poverty. At best, "the approach of relative deprivation supplements rather than supplants the analysis of poverty in terms of absolute dispossession".[44]

5. A Policy of Definition

All societies abhor the persistence of poverty and hence adopt their own 'norms' or 'standards' to identify, measure and formulate programmes for its alleviation:

> "If society believes that the people should not be permitted to die of starvation or exposure, then it will define poverty as the lack of minimum food and shelter necessary to maintain life. If society feels some responsibility for providing to all persons an established measure of well-being beyond mere existence, for example, good physical health, then it will add to its list of necessities the resources required to prevent or cure sickness. At any given time a policy definition reflects a balancing of community capabilities and desires. In low income societies the community finds it possible to worry much beyond physical survival other societies, more able to support their dependent citizens, begin to consider the effects that pauperism will have on the poor and nonpoor alike".[45]

One of the basic problems confronting this approach relates to the nexus between the policy and the polity and invokes an unending debate on "what should be done" and "what could be done" to eliminate poverty. Policy formulation inevitably involves "assessment of feasibilities" but the unfeasibility of elimination of specific deprivation must not be construed as absence of deprivation. Inescapable poverty is still poverty. Further, nature and content of state Policy are influenced by political considerations and may reflect aside from feasibility considerations, objectives other than poverty eradication.

Conclusion

It is held that characteristics of the poor are situational rather than cultural. Culture as a criteria to define poverty refers to the consequences of poverty for, poverty is not a trait but a condition. Deprivation is, indeed a central point in the concept of poverty but 'relative' deprivation explains poverty in appropriately for it ignores absolute dispossession as a 'core' of poverty. Emphasis to consider poverty as an issue in inequality is misplaced. Poverty and inequality are related to each other but neither subsumes the other. Policy definition of poverty displays political overtones and concedes a part of poverty because it is unfeasible to eliminate it. Widely criticised biological approach to define poverty needs to be refined rather than rejected for, it focuses attention on the critical issues of poverty—hunger and starvation. This approach with suitable refinements constitutes the basis of most of the studies on poverty aiming at its measurement and prescription of policies for its eradication.

References

1. Schultz, T.W., "Economic Crises in World" Agriculture"; University of Michigan Press, 1965, pp. 26-27.
2. Boulding, Kenneth, E., "Reflections on Poverty," New York Columbia University Press, 1961, p. 55.
3. Smolensky, E., "Investment in Education of the Poor"—American Economic Review Supplement LV, May, 1966.

4. Rein, Martin., "Problems in the definition and measurement of Poverty"—Concept of Poverty Ed. Townsend Heineman, London, 1970, pp. 46-47.
5. Titmuss, R., 'Income, Distribution and Social Change'. Allen and Unwin, London, 1962, p. 187.
6. Townsend, Peter, "Measures and Explanations of Poverty in High Income and Low Income Countries : The problems of operationalizing the concepts of development, class and poverty'—Ed. Concept of poverty—Allen and Unwin, London, 1963, pp. 1-45.
7. Lewis, Oscar, "The Culture of Poverty". On Understanding Poverty—Ed. Danial P. Moynihan—Basic Books Inc. Publishers, New York/London, 1968, pp. 187-88.
8. Rossi, Peter, H , and Blum, Zahava, D. "Class, Status and Poverty" in Maynihan, Daniel P. On Understanding Poverty—Basic Books Inc. Publishers, New York/London, 1968, pp. 38-39.
9. Lewis, Hylan, "Culture, Class and the Behaviour of low Income Families"—Culture, Class and Poverty Washington Cros-Tell, 1967, pp 17-18.
10. Gans, Herbert, "Culture and Class in the Study of Poverty in Moynihan, Daniel, P. ed. On Understanding Poverty, p. 216.
11. Duncan, Otis Dudely, "Inheritance of Race" In Moynihan, Daniel, P. Ed., p. 88.
12. Schultz, Theodore, W., "Investy in Poor people". An Economist View"—American Economic Review Vol. LV Nod, May 1965, p. 510.
13. Rauntree, B S., "Poverty and Progress : A Second Social Survey of York" London Longmans, Green, 1941, pp. 102-03.
14. Rauntree, B S., *op. cit*,, p. 103.
15. Rain Martin, *op. cit.*, p. 48.
16. Gadgil, D. R , "Sholapur City, Socio-Economic Studies"—Asia Publishing House, 1968, pp. 223-34.
17. Watts, Harrod, "An Economic Definition of Poverty"—In Moynihan Daniel, P. ed., pp. 316-22.
18. Luck, J. Murray, "The War on Malnutrition and Poverty", New York, Harper and Brothers, 1946, p. 15.
19. Rao, V.K.R.V., "Food nutrition and Poverty in India"—New Delhi, Vikas Publishing House, 1982, p. 138.
20. Orshansky, M., "Counting the Poor : Another look at the poverty profile, social security Bulletin, XXVIII, No. 1, January, 1965, p. 5.
21. Orshansky, M., *op. cit.*, p. 3.
22. Food and Agriculture Organisation, "Energy and Portain Requirements", Rome, 1973.
23. Rao, V.K.R.V., *op. cit.*, p. 38.

24. Food and Agriculture Commission. "Agricultural Commodity Projections, 1970-80", Rome, p. 31.
25. Dandekar, V. M., and Rath, Neelkanth. "Poverty in India" Indian School of Political Economy, Pune, 1971, p. 8.
26. Govens, James, D., and Nixon, John, A. "India—A perspective on the food front" in "Food, Politics, Economics, Nutrition and - Research", A sciance compendium American Association for the Advancement of science (ed) Philip Abelson, 1975, p. 50.
27. Planning Commission, Government of India. "Dwaft, five Year Plan 1978-83, Mimeographed, Vol. II, p. 36.
28. Acharya, K.T., "Invisible Fat intake from Indian Dietaries". The Indian Journal of Nutritional Diet, 13, 1976, pp. 363-70.
29. Sukhatme, P.V., "Incidence of Undernutrition" Indian Journal of Agriculture Economics, July-September, 1977, p. 7.
30. The Research and Planning Division of the Economic Commission on Asia and Far-East. "On the Measurement of Mass Poverty in India" Economic Bulletin for Asia and the Far East, Vol. XXIII, No. 3, Dec. 1972, pp. 63-64.
31. Engels Co-efficient, Explanation on.
32. Kuznets, Simon, "Quantitative Aspect of the Economic Growth of the Nations. VIII. Distribution of Income by Size" Economic Development and Cultural Change, Jan., 1963.
33. Cited by Beckar, Gary, S., and Chiswick, Barry, R. Rishi, "Education and the Distribution of Farmings" American Economic Review, Vol. LVI, No. 2, May, 1966, p. 358.
34. Miller, S.M., and Roby, Pamela, *op. cit.*, pp. 142-45.
35. Rein, Martin, *op. cit.*, p. 46.
36. Bhatty, I.Z., "Inequality and Poverty in Rural India", In T.N. Shrinivasan and P K. Bardham, eds. Poverty and Income Distribution in India, Calcutta. Statistical Publishing Society, 1974, p. 292.
37. Townsend, Peter, *Ibid.*, pp. 2, 19.
38. Townsend, Peter, *Ibid.*, p. 42.
39. Wedderburn, Dorothy (ed.) "Poverty, Inequality, and class structure". Cambridge University Press, 1974, pp. 15-16.
40. Atkinson, A.B., "The Economics of Inequality" Oxford University, Press, 1975, p. 186.
41. Wedderburn, Dorothy (ed.), *op. cit.*, p 4.
42. Townsend Peter, "Poverty as Relative Deprivation, Resource and Styles of living" in Poverty Inequality, structure, Wedderburn, *op. cit.*, pp. 25-26.
43. Dantwala, M.L, "Poverty in India : Then and Now : 1870-1970", The Macmillan Company of India, Ltd., Delhi, 1973.
44. Sen, A.K, "Poverty and Famines : An Essay on Entillement and Deprivation," Oxford University Press, Oxford, 1982, p. 17.

2

Measurement of Poverty

In the previous chapter it is neatly held that an ideal poverty identification measure should reflect a single definable, quantifiable characteristics that all poor families and only poor families should possess. However, due to varied perceptions of poverty, it is highly improbable to devise such a measure as could identify only those families or individuals as all would agree are poor. The level and structure of consumption since determines the extent of welfare, therefore poverty measures are ultimately related to ability to consume. Given the complex problems associated with the measurement of consumption and also the degree of ambiguity in the phrase 'ability to consume', the measurement of poverty has centered on adapting information on family income. The income approach to poverty at best explains the relative position of an individual or a family on a scale of income distribution and thus it gets related to relative deprivation. This measure does not take care of an irreducible minimum nutritional requirement necessary for sustenance/subsistence and therefore, in order to comprehend the minimum biological needs it is absolutely necessary to device some scientific measure of absolute deprivation. Precisely, the measurement of poverty is thus measured either with the help of some 'objective' criteria or a 'normative' norm, the former essentially measures inequality and the later absolute poverty.

Measures of Inequality

Measurement of income inequality has received considerable attention and elucidation over last couple of decades. As a consequence, refinements and modifications have been attempted to evolve some suitable measures or inequality. Some such measures are as under :

The Range :

Range is one of the simplest measures and is determined as under :—

Consider distribution of income over n persons, 1= 1,2... 2n and let y; be the income of person i. Let the average level of income be μ, so that :

$$\sum_{i=1}^{n} y_1 = n\mu \ldots\ldots\ldots\ldots(1)$$

The relative share of income going to person i is x_1. That is

$$y_1 = n^{\mu}x_1 \qquad \ldots\ldots\ldots\ldots(2)$$

The method is based on comparing the extreme value of distribution i.e., the highest and the lowest income levels. The range can be defined as the difference/gap between these two levels is the ratio of mean income. Thus, defined range E is given by :

$$E = [\text{Max } y_1 - \text{Min } y_1]/\mu \ldots\ldots\ldots\ldots(3)$$

If the income is divided absolutely equally than E=0. At the other extreme if one person receives all income, then E=n And E lies in general between O and n.

Range as a measure has got some advantages as it is very simple to calculate and easy to understand Wessel, Willett and Simone observe, "it (range) it still an important concept. Although it does not consider the measure in which the values are spread out within the distribution, but concerns itself only with the top and bottom values, the range is still an extremely useful measure". Again, it gives a broad picture of data in that it includes the limits within which all of the items occur.

The problem with the range as a measure is obvious as it is. Very much affected by the extreme items. Range is misleading if either of the extreme values is an unusual occurrence. It further does not provide, no other measure of the in-between values except that they lie between the two extreme values as is explained in the figure 1, below:

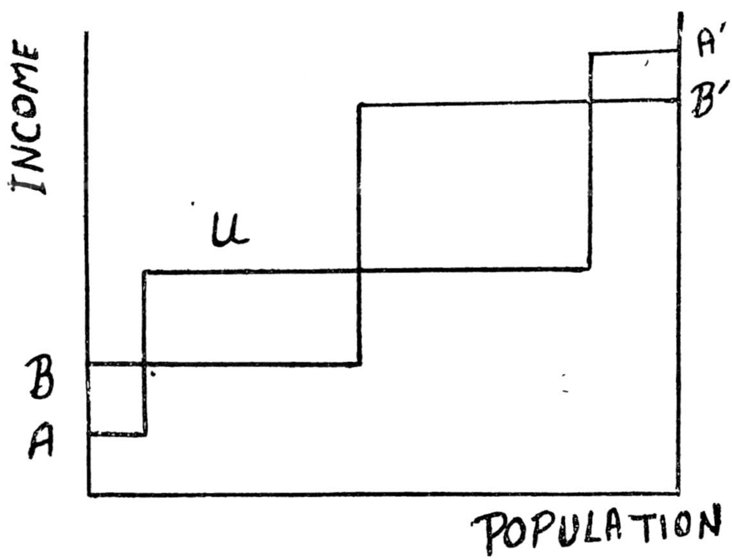

Fig 1.

The distribution AA′ has a wider range E that BB′, but most people under AA′ enjoy the mean income u with only a few aberrations. On the other hand BB′ involves a division of the population into two distinct classes of the rich and the poor. By concentrating on the extreme value only, the range misses important feature of contrast. Further, Range is influenced very much by fluctuations of sampling. In short, dependence on the two extreme items renders the range most unrealiable as a measure of the values within a distribution.

The Relative Mean of Deviation

To look at the entire distribution and not merely at the extreme values is to compare the income level of each with the mean income, to sum the absolute value of all the differences, and then to look at that sum as a proportion of total income. This yields the relative mean deviation M.

$$M = \sum_{i=1}^{n} /\mu - y_1/ = n\,\mu \ldots \qquad (4)$$

With perfect equality M=O and will all income going to one person only M=2 (n—1)/n. But unlike E, M takes note of entire distribution. For example in Fig. 1, the value of M is much higher for BB′ than for AA′ which corresponds to the notion of inequality.

This measure as in case of Range is simple and easy to understand. As Wessell, Willet and Simone state, "The outstanding feature/advantage of the mean deviation is its relative simplicity. Anyone familiar with the concept of average can readily appreciate the meaning of the average deviation. If a situation requires a measure, that will be presented to the general public or any group not thoroughly grounded in statistics, the average deviation is very useful". Mean deviation is a calculated value which is based on all the items and is less effected by the extreme values.

The main problem with the relative mean deviation is that it is not at all sensitive to transfer from a poorer person to a richer person as long as both lie on the same side of the mean income. Rupee one transferred from the poorest man to some one more rich but having less than the mean income would add to one gap and reduce another gap by exactly the same amount and since these gaps are simply added up in the process of arriving at M, this transfer would leave M completely unchanged.

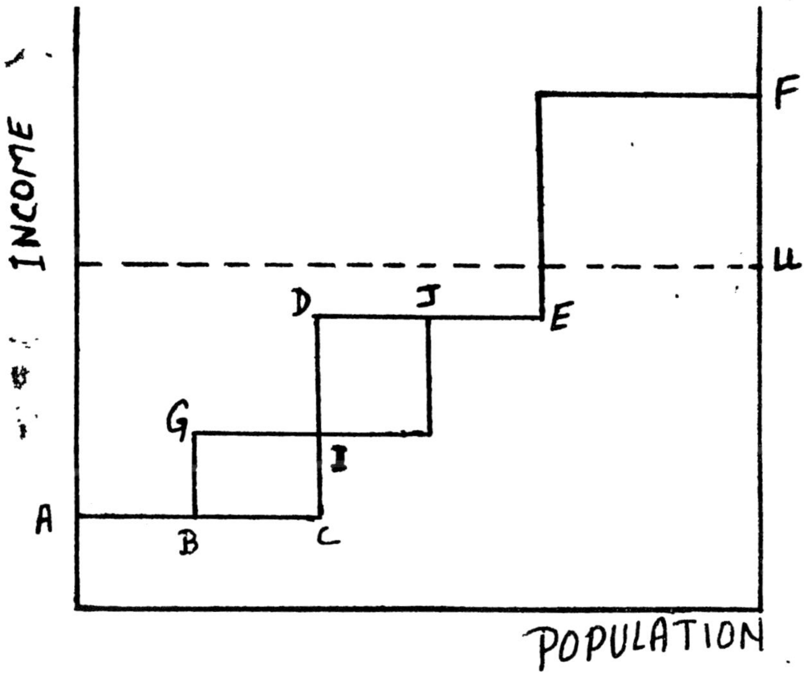

Fig 2.

In Fig. 2, the distribution ABCDEF is transformed into ABGHJEF by transferring income to some of the poorest from a richer class. But the value of M remains unchanged, since the diminution of the gap by BGIC is exactly compensated by the increase of the gap by DIHJ, since BC and DJ are equal and so are BG and JH. As a measure M seems to take no notice of income transfers whatsoever unless they cross the dividing line of u on the way. As a measure, M fails to catch the commonly accepted ideas on inequality which would tend to regard ABCDEF as more unequal than ABGHJEF.

The Variance and the Coefficient of Variation

Rather than simply adding the absolute values of the gaps, if we square them and then add, this would have the result of accentuating differences further away from the mean, so that a transfer like the one shown in Fig. 2 would reduce the inequality measure variance, the common statistical measure of variation, does have this property,

$$V = \sum_{i=1}^{n} (u-y_i)^2/n \ldots \quad \ldots \quad \ldots \qquad (5)$$

In Fig. 2, ABCDEF has a higher variance than ABGHJEF since in the process of squaring, BG has a stronger impact than JH. Any transfer from a poorer person to a richer person, other things remaining the same, always increases the variance and this is an attractive property for an inequality measure. In fact as early as 1920, Hugh Dalton had argued that any measure of inequality must have this minimal property and since in this Dalton was following a lead of Pigou, whom he quoted, hence this is called Pigou-Dalton condition.

However, the variance depends on the mean income level, and one distribution may show much greater relative variation than another and still end up having a lower variance if the mean income level around which the variations take place is smaller than with other distribution. A measure that does not have this deficiency and concentrates on relative variation is the coefficient of variation, which is the square root of the variance divided by the mean income level:

$$C = V^{\frac{1}{2}}/u \quad \ldots \quad \ldots \quad \ldots \quad \ldots \qquad (6)$$

While the co-efficient of variation captures the property of being sensitive to income transfers for all income levels and unlike the variance, is independent of the mean income level, the procedure of squaring the difference is a very particular one. It is easily checked that C does have the characteristic of attaching equal weights to transfers of income at different income levels i.e., the impact of a small transfer from a person with income 'y' to one with income (y—d) is the same irrespective of the value of y.

The Standard Deviation of Logarithms

Logarithms recommends itself that if one wishes to attach greater importance to income transfer at the lower end, a reasonable way of going about it is to take some transformations of incomes that staggers the income level. One other advantage of the logarithms in contrast with taking the variance or the standard deviation of actual values, is that it eliminates the arbitrariness of the units and therefore, of absolute levels, since a change of units which takes the form of a multiplication of the absolute values, comes out in the logarithmic form as an addition of a constant, and therefore goes out when pairwise differences are being taken. It is, therefore, no wonder that the standard deviation of the logarithm has frequently cropped up as a suggested measure of inequality. The deviation is taken from the geometric mean rather than from the arithmetic mean, but in the income distribution literature using the arithmetic mean seems more common (Atkinson, 1970; Stark, 1972).

$$H = \left[\sum_{i=1}^{n} (\log^{\mu} - \log y_i)^2 / n \right]^{\frac{1}{2}} \qquad \text{.........(7)}$$

The fact that a logarithmic transformation staggers the income levels tends to soften the blow in reflecting inequality since it reduces the deviation, but on the other hand it has the property of highlighting differences at the lower end of the scale. But since income levels, as they get higher and higher, suffer increasingly severe contraction, this makes H as a measure of welfare not concave at all at high income levels. If one wants social welfare to be a concave function of individual incomes then H as a measure of inequality can cause problems, despite attractive features in other respects.

The Gini Coefficient

A measure that has been very widely used to represent the extent of inequality is the Gini-co-efficient attributed to Gini (1912) and much analysed by Ricci (1916) and later by Dalton (1920) Yniema (1938), Atkinson (1970), Newbery (1970), Sheshinshi (1972) and others. Corrando Ginni an Italian statistician, has suggested that instead of measuring from any measure i.e., mean, range, variance, the mean differences between the values of all possible pairs of the variable should be found out, and it would result in good measure. Thus, this measure is equal to the mean difference of each possible pair of the values of the variable.

Symbolically :

$$\text{Ginni's mean} = \frac{g}{m}$$

Where g stands for the total of the differences in the values of all possible pairs of a variable and m stands for the total number of differences. The total number of differences would be equal to $\frac{1}{2}n\ (n-1)$.

The sensitivity of Ginni-coefficient depends not on the size of the income levels but on the number of people in between them, The Ginni co-efficient implies a welfare function which is just a weighted of different people's income level with the weights being determined by the rank order position of the person in the ranking by income levels. But the actual weights would depend upon precisely how the population is distributed over income sizes. Ginni co-efficient does not imply a strictly concave group welfare functions. The welfare function must be thought to be—G, since a higher value of Gini-coefficient (G) shows greater inequality, which corresponds to less welfare. It is—G that is concave but not strictly Ginni Co-efficient is a linear function of income levels. The validity of this property has been questioned recently by a number of scholars. Atkinson (1970) questioned the Ginni co-efficient's lack of strict concavity. Newbery concluded that no additive social welfare function based on strictly concave individual utility functions can order to the distribution of a given total in precisely the opposite order to the ranking of the values of the Gini Co-efficients. The Gini-coefficient is more opaque since it measures the distance between the diagonal "line of equal distribution" and the Lorenz curve. Unlike the Lorenz comparisons, the Gini-co-efficient comparisons are always conclusive since one real number must be greater than, equal to or less than another Gini-co-efficient can be written as:

$$G = (1/2n^2 \mu) \sum_{i=1}^{n} \sum_{j=1}^{n} /y_i - y_j/$$

$$= 1 - \frac{1}{n^2\mu} \sum_{i=1}^{n} \sum_{j=1}^{n} \text{Min } y_1 - y_2$$

$$= 1 + \frac{1}{n} - \frac{2}{n^2\mu}(y_1 + y_2 + \ldots y_n)$$

for $y_1 \geqslant y_2 \geqslant y_3 \ldots\ldots \geqslant y_n$

In taking differences over all pairs of incomes, the Gini-Co-efficient or the absolute mean difference avoids the total concentration on differences vis-a-vis the mean which C, V or H has. In avoiding the arbitrary squaring procedure of C, V or H, it may seen to be a more direct approach as well, without sacrificing the quality of being sensitive to transfers from the rich to the poor at every level. Undoubtedly, one appeal of the Gini Co-efficient or the relative mean difference, lies in the fact that it is very direct measure of income difference, taking note of differences between every pair of incomes.

Lorenz Curve

The Lorenz curve is a graphical method of showing deviation from the average of a group of data. This method with the help of curves was devised by Dr. Marx O. Lorenz, a famous economist. He used this technique for measuring the distribution of wealth and income.

The Lorenz curve is a device used to show the concentration of ownership of economic quantities, such as income and wealth. If the cummulative distribution of the amount of the variable of income is plotted as the ordinate against the comulative frequency distribution of the individuals possessing the amount plotted as the abscissa, the resultant curve is a Lorenz curve. Lorenz curve is based upon the assumption that in case of equal distribution the curve will be a straight line.

The Lorenz Curve shows the percentage of income received by the bottom x per cent of the population with x varying from 0 to 100. The great advantage of Lorenz Curve comparisions is that "we can say something about comparative levels of social welfare without specifying anything very particular about the extent of welfare function" as long as the welfare function "is a symmetric and strictly quasi-concave function of the vector of individual incomes" without knowing anything about the nature of social welfare functien w(.), we can say that a higher Lorenz Curve implies more social welfare for the same total of income. Thus a higher Lorenz Curve implies a more equal distribution is strictly objective (rather than normative) sense. If we compare two distributions, and Lorenz Curve of one is uniformly above that of another, Lorenz Curve will suffice as far as inequality measurement is concerned.

In Lorenz Curve the size of items and the frequencies are both cumulated and taking the total as 100, percentage are calculated for the various cumulated values. If there is proportionately each distribution of the frequencies over the various values of a variate, the points would lie in a straight line. This line is called the "Line of Equal Distribution". If the distribution of items is not proportionately equal, it indicated variability and the curve would be away from the line of equal distribution. The further the curve is from this, the greater is the variability in series. Fig. 3 Lorenz Curve B

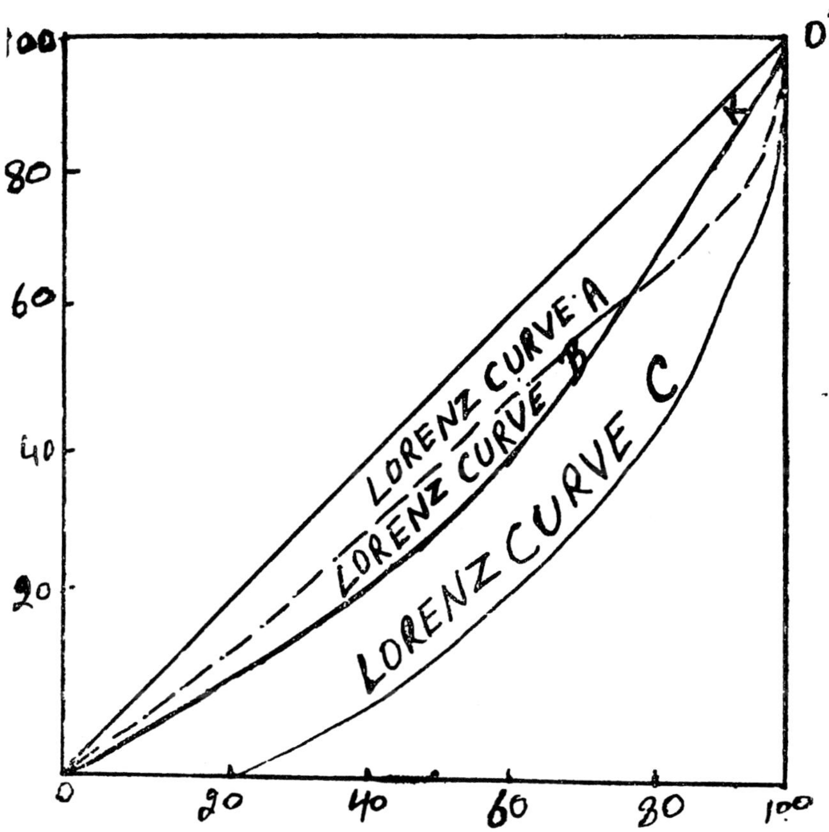

Commulative Percentage of Population (Fig 3.)

shows comparatively more equal distribution of income to that of Lorenz Curve C.

If we compare two distributions and the Lorenz Curve of one is uniformly above that of another, we are in luck as far as inequality measurement is concerned. Even if the total income varies, we can say that the change from the first to the second involves an inequality increasing shift in the distribution of income combined with a change in total income. But sometimes two distributions do not have this property and the Lorenz Curve may cross. However, the moment the Lorenz Curve of the two distributions intersect, one faces the more fundamental limitation of the Gini-Co-efficient, for it is no more possible to make any judgement about the relative welfare implications of the two distributions. Depending on how the two curves intersect, one of them may represent a superior welfare position even when the Gini-Co-efficient of both distribution is the same. In Fig. III, Lorenz Curve A starts below Curve B from O to K and rise above it later from K to O. A good example of the type is given by two alternative estimates of the distribution of rural consumption in 1964-65 based respectively on the National Sample Survey data and the data of the National Council of Applied Economic Research. The NCAER Lorenz Curve starts above the NSS Curve but falls below it later.

The main drawback of Lorenz Curve is, it does not give any quantitative/numerical value of the extent of inequality, It merely gives a picture of the extent to which a series is pulled away from an equal dirtribution. It serves as a supplement and should be used along with some quantitative measure of inequality.

Theil's Entropy Measure

Another measure of inequality has been proposed by Theil (1967), derives from the notion of entropy in information theory and is in terms of motivation. He argues:

when X is the probability that a certain event will occur, the information content h(X) of noticing that the event has in fact occurred must be decreasing function of X — the more unlikely event. One formula that satisfies this property is the logarithm of the reciprocal of X.

$$h(X) = \log (1/X) \text{ ....} \qquad (1)$$

When there are 'n' possible events, 1, ...n we take the respective probabilities X_1, X_1 . . . . .X_n such that

$X_1 \geqslant O$ and $\sum_{i=1}^{n} X_1 = 1$. The entropy or the expected information content of the situation can be sum of the information content of each event weighted by the respective probabilities.

$$H(X) = \sum_{i=1}^{n} X_1 h(X_1)$$

$$= \sum_{i=1}^{n} X_1 \log \left(\frac{1}{X_1}\right) \qquad \text{......} (2)$$

It is clear that the closer the 'n' probabilities X_1 are to (1/n), the greater is the entropy. If X_1 is interpreted as the share of income going to person i, H(X) is a measure of equality. When each X_1 equals (1/n), H(X) attains its maximum value of log n. If we subtract the entropy H(X) of an income distribution from its maximum value of log n, we get an index of inequality. This is Theil's measure.

$$T = \log n - H(X)$$

$$= \sum_{i=1}^{n} X_1 \log nX_1 \qquad \text{......} (3)$$

A shift from a richer to a poorer person lowers T i.e., it satisfies the Pigou-Dalton condition.

Dalton's Measure

In a classic contribution, Dalton (1920) argued that any measure of economic inequality must be concerned with economic welfare to be of relevance. The particular measure that he chose followed directly from the utilitarian frame-work, and he based it on a comparison between actual levels of aggregate utility and the level of total utility that would obtain if income were equally divided. Since he took a strictly concave utility function, i.e., with diminishing marginal utility of income and the same function for all, the maximization of aggregate welfare required an equal division. Dalton took the ratio of actual social welfare to the maximal social welfare as his measure of equality, taking the utility levels to be all positive.

$$D = \left[\sum_{i=1}^{n} U(y_1) \right] / n\,U(\mu) \ldots\ldots (1)$$

Atkinson (1970) has pointed out that this measure suffers from the difficulty that it is not invariant with respect to positive linear transformations of the utility function, conditional utility implies that any positive linear transformation would do just as well and Dalton's measure takes arbitrary values depending on which particular transformation is chosen.

Atkinson's Measure

Atkinson defines what he calls the 'equally distributed equivalent income' of a given distribution of a total income, and this is defined as that level of per capita income which if engaged by everybody would make total welfare exactly equal to the total welfare generated by the actual income distribution. Putting y_e as 'the equally distributed equivalent income', we have

$$y_e = y \left[n\,U(y) \right] = \sum_{i=1}^{n} U(y_1) \ldots\ldots (2)$$

The sum of the actual welfare levels of all equals the welfare sum that would emerge if everyone had y_e income Since each U(y) is taken to be concave i,e., with non-increasing marginal utility, y_e cannot be larger than the mean income u. Further, it can be shown that the more equal the distribution the closer will y_e be to u. Atkinson's measure of inequality is

$$A = 1 - (y_e/u) \ldots\ldots \qquad \ldots(3)$$

Obviously if income is equally distributed than y_e is equal to u and the value of Atkinson's measure will be zero. For any distribution the value of A must be between O and 1.

There are some difficulties with Atkinson's measure as he requires that the function U(y) be concave, but not necessarily strictly concave, i.e., U′ O and U″ O. Consider two distribution between two persons with a given total amount of income say (0, 10) and (5, 5). If we choose a I(y) function such that it is proportional to y, both will have precisely the same Atkinson measure of inequality.

Atkinson concluded that:

(1) The use of variance implies increasing inequality aversion, all the other measures (i.e., the co-efficient of variatian, the relative mean deviation, the Gini co-efficient and the standard deviation of logarithms imply constant (relative) inequality aversions.

(2) The relative mean deviation is not strictly cancave and is not sensitive to transfers on the same side of the mean.

(3) The co-efficient of variation attaches equal weight to transfers at different income levels, the Gini Co-efficient attaches more weight to transfers affecting middle income classes and the standard deviation weights transfers at the lower and more heavily.

Head Count Measure

The commenest measure of over all poverty is the head count measure H, given by the proportion of the total population that happens to be identified as poor, e.g., as falling below the specified poverty line income. If 'q' is the number of people who are identified as being poor and is the total number of people in the community, then the head-count measure is q/n.

$$H = \frac{q}{n}$$

This index has been widely used—explictly or by implication—ever since quantitative study and measurement of poverty began (Booth, 1889; Rountree, 1901). It is still the mainstay of poverty statistics on which poverty programmes are based (Orshansky, 1965, 1966; Abel Smith and Townsend, 1965). It has been extensively utilised recently both for inter-temporal as well as for international comparisons.

The head-count measure, H is not insensitive to the number below the poverty line; indeed, for a given society it is the only thing to which H is sensitive. But H pays no attention whatever to the extent of income short-fall of those who lie below the poverty line. It is immaterial whether someone is just below the line or very far from it, in acute misery and hunger.

Furthermore, a transfer of income from a poor person to one who is richer can never increase the poverty measure H. The poor person from whom the transfer takes place is, in any case, counted in the value of H, and no reduction of his income will make him count any-more then he does already. On the other hand, the person who receives the income transfer cannot of course, move below the poverty line as a consequence of this. Either he was rich and stays so or was poor and stays so, in both of which cases the H measure remains unaffected; or he was below the line but is pulled above it by the transfer, and this makes the measure H fall rather than rise. So a transfer from a poor person to one who is richer can never increase poverty as represented by H.

There are, thus, good grounds for rejecting the standard poverty measures in terms of which most of the analyses and debates on poverty have traditionally taken place. The head-count measure in particular has commanded implicit support of a kind that is quite astonishing Consider A.L. Bowley's (1923) famous assertion: "There is, perhaps, no better test of the progress of the nation, than which shows what proportion are in poverty". The spirit of the remark is acceptable enough, but surely enough not the gratuitous identification of poverty with the head count measure H.

Income-Gap Ratio

Another measure that has had a fair amount of currency is the 'poverty gap, which is the aggregate short-fall of income of all the poor from the poverty line. The index can be normalized by being expressed as the percentage short-fall of the average income of the poor from the poverty line. This measure-denoted, I—is called the 'Income-gap-ratio'.

If 'q' is the number of people who are identified as poor, g is the total poverty gap of the poor and π is the poverty line, then Income Gap I is

$$I = \frac{g}{q\pi}$$

The income-gap ratio I is completely insensitive to transfers of income among the poor so long as no body crosses the poverty by such transfers. It also pays no attention whatever to the number or proportion of poor people below the poverty line, concentrating only on the aggregate short falls, no matter how it is distributed and among how many. These are damaging limitations.

COMBINATION OF THESE POVERTY MEASURES

The Head Count and Income Gap Ratio

The head-count measure H ignores the extent of income-short-falls, while the income gap-ratio I ignores the numbers involved. However, this is still inadequate if a unit of income is transferred from a person below the poverty line to someone who is richer but who still is below the poverty line, then both the measure H and I will remain completely unaffected. Hence any 'combined' measure based only on these two must also show no response whatsoever to such a change, despite the obvious increase in aggregate poverty as a consequence of this transfer in terms of relative deprivation.

This is, however, special case in which a combination of H and I might just be adequate. While individually H is insensitive to the extent of income short-falls and I to the numbers involved, the combination of two can be criticised on the ground, for this insensitivity to variations of distribution of income among the poor. If we confine only to all the poor have precisely same income, then H & I combination may be adequate.

Axiomatic Derivation of a Poverty Measure 'P'

Poverty can be conceived of as a weighted sum of the poverty gaps of the poor. This can be done with weights that can be functions of other variables. To base the poverty measure on some quantification of the sum total loss of utility arising from the penury of the poor, then weights should be derived from the familiar utilitarian considerations. If it is assumed that utility of each person depends only on the income of the other. But this use of the traditional utilitarian model will miss the idea of relative deprivation—which is central to the nation of poverty. Further, difficulties with such cardinal comparisons of utility gains and losses even if we ignore these, it becomes little difficult to secure agreement on using one particular utility function among so many postulated, all satisfying the usual regularity conditions (such as diminishing marginal utility).

The approach used in the derivation of measure P can be justified either by bringing in the notion of personal welfare conceived in ordinal terms or by directly axiomalizing on income distribution. In this case, a simples and directly income-based format will be employed.

Conceiving poverty as a weighted sum of the poverty gaps of poor.

$$P = A(n, q, \pi) \sum_{i \in T} V_i g_i$$

where V_i = weight of poverty gap g_i of person i

$A(n, q, \pi)$ = normalising parameter dependent on the total number of people n the number of poor people q and the poverty line π

It has also not been specified that V_i must depend only on the size of person i's poverty gap or income level y_i. Also it may be reasonable to agree of the weight V_i of the poverty gap of i to be dependent on i's relative position vis-a-vis others in the reference group. Also V_i can be made an increasing function of r(i) so that the weights depend on. Where i stands in the ranking vis-a-vis other people. The case of such an increasing function is the identify mapping.

$$m = f(m)$$

Ranked Relative Deprivation (Axiom R)

Poverty is measured with the weight V_i on person i's poverty gap equally is income rank among the poor.

$$V_i = r(i).$$

Let r(i) be the rank of person i in the ordering of all the poor in the decreasing order of income, e.g. r(i)=12. If i is the twelfth worst off among the poor. If more than one person has the same income, they can be ranked in any arbitrary order the poverty measure much be such that it should not matter which particular arbitrary order is chosen among those with the same income. The poorest poor has the largest rank value 'q' when there are q people altogether on this side of poverty line, while the least poor has the rank value I. The greater the rank value, the more the person is deprived in terms of relative deprivation with respect to the others in the same category. It is thus reasonable to argue that a poverty measure capturing this aspect of relative deprivation must make the weight on a persons income short fall increase with the rank value.

This axiom of Ranked Relative (Axiom R) focuses on the distribution of income among the poor, and may be combined with the kind of information that is presented by the head count measure H and income gap ratio I in the special case in which everyone below the poverty line has the same income H represents, the proportion of people who are deprived in relation to property line and I reflects the proportionate amount of absolute income deprivation vis-a-vis that line. It can further be said that H (how much) catches one aspect of overall deprivation and I catches another aspect (How many). In special cases when all the poor have the same income H and I together, it gives an account of extent of poverty in terms of overall deprivation. Since the problem of relative distribution among the poor does not arise in this special case. A representation of this, leads to a convenient normalisation is the product HI. This is called axion of 'Normalized Absolute Deprivation' (Axiom A).

$$\text{If for all } 16T;\ y_1 = y^*, \text{ then}$$

$$P = HI$$

For large numbers of the poor, the only poverty measure satisfying Axioms R and A is given by:

$$P = H\,[I + (1-I)G]$$

Where G is the Gini co-efficient of income distribution among the poor.

Putting $g^* = g_i$ for all i we get

$$P = \frac{1}{2}\,[A(n, q, \pi),\; g^*\, q\,(q+1)]$$

Combining with the following equation:

$$H = q/n$$
$$I = g^*/\Pi$$
$$P = HI$$

and this results in:

$$A(n, q, \pi) = 2/(q+1)n\pi$$

Again combining the following equation:

$$V_i = r(i)$$
$$P = A(n, q, \pi)\Sigma V_i g_i$$
$$A(n_1 q_1 \pi) = 1/(q+1)n\pi$$

and we obtain the following equation.

$$P = \frac{2}{(q+1)n\,\pi} \sum_{r(i)=1}^{q} (\pi - y_i)\, r(i)$$

Now Gini co-efficient for any q member population with mean income y^* and income ranks $r(i) = 1, 2 \ldots q$, can be written as

$$G = 1 + \frac{1}{q} - \frac{2}{q^2 y^*} \sum_{r(i)=1}^{q} y_i\, r(i)$$

and further simplications yield

$$P = H\,[1-(1-I)\,[1-Gq)/(q+1)]$$

For large q above equation is reduced to

$$P = H\,[I+(1-I)\,G]$$

An alternative expression of P can be obtained by eliminating I and replacing it by its equivalent $(1-y^*/n)$ and this procedure, discussed by Anand (1977), yields:

$$P = H\,[1-y^*\,(1-G)/\pi]$$

A dilierent generalisation based on a reinterpretation of the poverty Index P has been proposed by Blackorby and Donaldson (1980). They note that the measure P can be seen as the product of the head-count ratio H and the proportions gap between the poverty line income π and the Atkinsons—Kolm' equally distributed equivalent income' (eg) of the incomes of the poor when the evaluation is done with the Gini social evalution function.

$$P = H\,(\pi - eg)/\pi$$

$$eg = y^{*}\,(1 - G)$$

If the social evaluation function is changed, a new poverty measure would emerge corresponding, with the equally distributed equivalent income defined according to that social evaluation function.

$$P = H\,(\pi - e)/\pi$$

Blackorby and Donaldson chose an ethical interpretation of the poverty measures. The value of a reflects that level of income which, if shared by all the poor, would be judged by the social evalution function to be exactly as good as the actual distribution of income among the poor. But it easily noticed that the format permits a descriptive interpretation as well viz., standing for that level of income which if shared by all the poor will be regarded as displaying as much over-all poverty as the actual distribution of income among the poor.

Another interesting variant of the poverty measure P has been proposed by Takayama (1979) related to an approach that has been extensively explored by Hamada and Takayama (1978). From the actual income distribution a 'censured' income distribution is obtained by replacing the income that exceed the poverty line by incomes exactly equally the poverty line (π), Takayama (1979) then takes the Gini-Co-efficient G_o of the censured income distribution as the measure of poverty. Other measures of inequality are also applied to the censured distribution to derive corresponding measures of poverty in Hamada and Takayama (1978).

The approach has some clear merits. The Gini co-efficient of the censured distribution is a very close substitute of Gini measure of inequality into a poverty measure. It doctors the income distribution itself by ignoring the information on the actual incomes of the people who are not poor, but counts them in with poverty line incomes. Takayama (1979) has also provided abiomatizations of his measure of poverty G_c and Hamada and Takayama (1978) have suggested deviations for similar poverty measures based on inequality indexes applied to the censured distribution.

The main drawback of this approach lies in its robust violation of the monotonicity axiom viz., that a reduction of income of anyone below the poverty line given everything else, must increase the poverty measure. A person below the poverty line may still be among the relatively richer in the censured distribution of income with an income above the mean and median of that distribution. A reduction of his income will in an obvious sense reduce the extent of inequality in the censured distribution, but in an equally obvious sense the community must now be having more poverty. So the simplicity of the formulae used by Takayama (1979) and Hamada and Takayama (1978) is achieved at some real cost, dropping the monotonic relation between the poverty measure and vector-dominance of deprivation of the poor.

Problems in the Measurement of Poverty

There are number of problems associated as far as the measurement aspect of poverty is concerned. Some of the problems are listed below:

First, there are the short-comings of the basic data source. Data is normally derived from a small sample of the population (about 1 person in 2,500), so that, for instance year to year changes in the estimates may be attributable to sampling fluctuations. It does not cover people not living in households thus excluding groups who may be particularly vulnerable, such as the homeless and those in institutions. There is a sizeable degree of non-response (around 30 per cent), so that the estimates may be effected by differential non-response by different groups. There is evidence that certain types of income are understated when the survey totals are grossed up and compared with the national accounts aggregates. These considerations must be borne in mind when assessing the estimates. At the same time, the impact of these short-comings should not be exaggerated. For example, a detailed study/investigation of the understatement of income (Atkinson and Mickle Wright, 1983) concluded that this was associated mainly with the investment income and self-employment income, which may be less relevant to the low income families considered and that for other more relevant types of income, such as earnings social security benefits and occupational pensions.

Second, there is the question of the definition of the unit, the supplementary benefit assessment is based on the family unit. On the other hand, a number of investigators, including Abel-Smith and townsend, have used the household definition. With such a broader unit, the proportion in poverty will tend to be lower, and the choice between them depends on the degree of income-sharing that takes place. As is put by Beckerman and Clark:

> "Whether the 'true' measure lies nearer one extreme or the other depends on the genuine amount of sharing of resources that takes place within any household or family unit. If there is none, for example, then the narrow unit would provide a correct estimate of poverty, since poor units would not be helped out by transfer of resources from richer units within the same household. If, on the other hand, there is full sharing, then the narrow unit would exaggerate poverty".

Beckerman and Clark go on to argue that the household

is 'probably preferable, since it is highly likely that in most multiple unit households there is enough intra-household sharing to prevent sub-units from falling below the poverty line.

Third, there are issues associated with the choice of period, when considering the incidence of poverty, we may want to take a short assessment period; we may be conceived with weekly income and here again referring to FES, one important instance the official estimates depart from current weekly income where the need of the family has been off work, through sickness as unemployment for less than thirteen weeks the official calculation is based not on these current income but on the family's normal income when the head is in work. This typically has the effect of reducing the number estimated to be in poverty.

The fourth question concerns the choice of poverty measure and which have been referred solely to the number below the poverty line or what has been called the head-count' measure, and this is the indicator that has been almost universally employed. This may appear quite surprising in view of the extensive research on the choice of measures of income inequality, but untill the contribution of Sen (1976) there was almost a complete divorce between the two literatures, it is evident that the head count ratio is not fully satisfactory. In particular, 'an unchanged number of people below the "poverty line" may go with a sharp rise in the extent or the short-fall of income from the poverty line'.

One way in which the extent of the short-fall can be incorporated is through the calculation of the 'poverty gap' in other words, to add the cash amounts by which people fall below the scale.

Finally, there is the choice of poverty standard. The use of the supplementary benefit scale is open to question. For example, there are the issues raised by inflation. The official estimates compare each family's income with the benefit scale applicable at the date of interview, taking no account of the fact that the scale is up-rated for inflation only once a year. Thus the Smith family interviewed on 5th November could be above the poverty line, but the Jones family interviewed two weeks later could be 10 per cent below the line, even though they both had exactly the same incomes and circumstances. At times of relatively rapid inflation this could make quite a difference.

References

1. Ahluwalia, M., "Rural Poverty in India, 1956-57 to 1973-74" in India Occasional Papers, World Bank Staff Working Papers, The World Bank, Washington, DC, Nov., 1978.
2. Ahmad, M. and Bhattacharyya, N. (1974), "Size Distribution of Per Capital Personal Income in India, 1955-56 to 1960-61 and 1963-1964" in Srinivasan, T.N. and Bardhan, P.K. (ed.), "Poverty and Income Distribution ın India", Statistical Publishing Society, Calcutta.
3. Anand, Sudhir, "Inequality and Poverty in Malayasia: Measurement and Decomposition Published for the World Bank by Oxford University Press.
4. Atkınson, A.B., "On the Measurment of Inequality", Journal of Economic Theory, vol. 2, (September, 1970), pp. 244-260.
5. Awasthi, G.D., Advanced Economic Statistics and Econometrics, Prakashan Kendra, Lucknow (1977).
5. Chiang, A.C., "Fundamental Methods of Mathematical Economics", McGraw Hill, Kogaknsha, Ltd.
7. Cramer, H., "Mathematical Methods of Statistics", Princeton University Press, Princeton.
8. Dandekar, V.M. and Rath, N. (1971), "Poverty in India", Economic and Political Weekly, vol. VI, Nos. 1 & 2.
9. Dandekar, V.M. (1981), "On Measurement of Poverty", Economic and Political Weekly, vol. XVI, No. 30.
10. Dandekar, V.M. (1982), "On Measurement of Under-nutrition", Economic and Political Weekly, vol. XVII, No. 6.
11. Goulden, C.H., Methods of Statistical Analysis, Asia Publishing House, 1962.
12. Gupta, B.N., "Statistics (Theory and Practice", Sahitya Bhawan, Agra, 1978.
13. Gupta, C.B., "In Introduction to Statistical Methods, Vikas Publishing House, Pvt. Ltd., (1979).

14. Gupta, S.C., "Fundamental of Statistics", Himalaya Publishing House, Bombay, (1981).
15. Gupta, S.C., "Statistical Methods", Sultan Chand and Sons, New Delhi, (1986).
16. Hebden, Julia, "Statistics for Economists", Philip Allan Publishers, Ltd., Oxford, (1981).
17. Iyengar, N.S. and Jain, L.R. (1974), "A Method of Estimating Income Distribution", Economic and Political Weekly, Vol. IX, No. 51.
18. Kakwani, N., "On a Class of Poverty Measures", Econometrica, Vol. 48, No. 2, March, 1980.
19. Krishanji, N. (1981), "On Measuring the Incidence of Undernutrition. A note on Sukhatme's Porcedure", Economic and Political Weekly, Vol. XVI, No. 22.
20. Krishanji, N. (1981), "On Measuring Incidence of Uundernutrition. What is a Consumer Unit", Economic and Political Weekly, Vol. XVI, No. 37.
21. Mode, E.B., "Elements of Statitics Prentice Hall", Ing. Englewood Cliffs, New Jersey.
22. Rao, V.K.R.V. (1981a), "Some Nutritional Puzzles : A Note", Economic and Political Weekly, Vol. XVI, Nos. 28-29.
23. Rao, V.K.R V. (1981b), "Measurement of Poverty : A Note", Economic and Political Weekl, Vol. XVI, No. 35.
24. Sen, A.K. (1973), "On Economic Inequality", Oxford University Press, Bombay.
25. Srinivasan, T.N., and Bardhan, P.K. (ed.) (1974), "Poverty and Income Distribution in India", Statistical Publishing Society, Calcutta.
26. Sukhatme, P.V. (1981), Measuring the Incidence of Undernutrition : A Comment Economic and Political Weekly, Vol. XVI, No. 32.
27. Thon Dominique : "A Poverty Measure", The Indian Economic Journal, Vol. 30, April-June, 1983, No. 4.

3

Incidence of Poverty in India

Historically, there is ample evidence in ancient literature to suggest that the phenomenon and pains of poverty were not unknown to Indians. However, due to the absence of systematic and authentic record of economic conditions in ancient India, opinion among economic historians about the nature of 'material' life enjoyed by the people reflect wide divergence. Historians like M.A. Buch (1922)[1], N.C. Bandhopodhay (1925)[2] and S.K. Das (1929)[3] have opined that economic conditions in ancient India were better than those of their own times. Ghoshal made a serious study of the taxation systems of India from the Vedic age to A.D. 1200 and stated that 'there is little, if any positive evidence, to prove that the burden of taxation in ancient and medieval periods was so heavy as to leave the cultivator a bare margin for subsistence".[4] In another study 'The Agrarian System in Ancient India" Ghoshal States, "...the glimpses which the observations of the foreign travellers furnish into the actual condition of the people generally indicate a happy and contended peasantry".[5] Following the publication of the full text of Arthshastra of Kautilya in 1909, historians nationalist have regarded the ancient period of Indian history as one of considerable prosperity and general contentments. Altekar while analysing the rural economy of western India in the early centuries before and after the Christian era asserted that "the people were better off than they are at present".[6] Morris and Stein contended these opinions and observed that 'the patriotic bias (in the writings of nationalists historians) often resulted in an exaggeration of the self-sufficiency of the early Indian Village out of all proportion and greater emphasis on the socially productive aspects of the corporate institutions (caste included) of the Pre-British India than warranted by available historial evidence.[7] Basu also arrived at the identical conclusions when he emphasized that "they (nationalist historian) often tried to cover up the social inequalities characteristic of the early Indian society by vague philosophical platitude".[8] In contrast to the nationalist historians, Bose had tried to show that "all was not well with the ancient economic system and that according to Jataka stories the peasants were exploited by the Princes".[9] Observations of Sharma on early Indian feudalism that, "the economic essence of Indian feudalism, like that of European, lay in the rise of landed intermediaries leading to the ensurement of the peasantry through mounting tax burdens, increasing obligations to perform forced labour and the evils of subinfeudation".[10] have lent powerful support to the ideas that the peasantry in India during early period was not free from exploitation. Besides, absence of growth factors was noticed in the village communities of ancient India when as early as 1817 James Mill asserted that Indian society has remained substantially unchanged since its inception.[11] Maity also concluded that as regards the material life of the common people, the Gupta period was not a golden age.[12] For the subsequent period, Pushpa Niyogi does not find any evidence to prove that the population as a whole was prosperous.[13] L. Gopal in one of his studies covering the period A.D, 700-1200 repeatedly suggests that the common people were far from happy and economically well off.

Opinions regarding economic conditions of the common people during Mughal period reveal that the prosperty of the nation was by and large maintained throughout the rule of Akbar, Jehangir and Shahjehan, but it come to a standstill when in Aurangzeb's reign, the incessant wars and the loss of human life paralysed agriculture, industry and trade. According to Hamilton, "In the best days of the Mughal Empire there was indeed a greater degree of prosperity than that of the previous era as also of the days which witnessed the decline of its power".[15] It is widely believed that with the closing years of the reign of Aurangzeb, the economic prosperity of India deteriorated as a natural sequal to the disappearance of peace and order. "Thus ensured", observes the historian of Aurangzeb, "a great economic improverishment of India, not only a decrease of the 'national stock', but also a rapid lowering of mechanical skill and standard of civilisation, a disappearance of art and culture over wide tracts of the country".[16] Majumdar and others observed, "it is certain that there was no golden age of opulence for the common people under the Mughals, because though the prices of articles were cheap, their average income was proporationately low or perhaps lower. They did not, however, grovel in misery and smart under discontent as their needs were few and the problems of life were not so complicated as those of the present day".[17]

These historical accounts unmistakenly reveal that India had attained a high level of development and the people under normal circumstances were not grinding under poverty and misery. Report of Indian Industrial Commission (1918) has lent support to this view by recording, "At a time when the west of Europe, the birth place of the modern industrial system, was inhabited by uncivilised tribes. India was famous for the wealth of her rulers and for the high artistic skill of her craftsmen. And even at a much later period, when merchant adventures from the west made their first appearance in India, the industrial development of this country was at any rate, not inferior to that of the more advanced European nations".[18]

Poverty During British Rule

With the British dominance over India, a parasitical symbiosis got established between an advanced trading (later on Industrial) nation and a vast agrarian state. In such a symbiosis Britain became strong and prosperous while as India was reduced to the status of a weak and poor country. This observation is supported by the terribly poor conditions of nourishment in India as against Britain in 1938-39 as summed up by Desai in the following table.[19]

Table 1

Distribution of Expenditure (Percentage)

Group	*India (1938-39)*	*England (1938)*
(a) Food	60.5	30.1
(b) Housing	6.0	21.5
(c) Other	33.5	58.4

Source: Desar, R.C., "Consumer Expenditure in India, 1931-32 to 1940-41", Journal of the Royal Statistical Society Series, Vol. CXI, Part 4, 1948, p. 277.

India's Expenditure structure with spending on food was twice as high as in England and about one half on housing indicated palpably low living standard in the country. Further investigation of the expenditure made by Desai from 1931-32 to 1940-41 at 1938-39 prices showed that living standard in India was declining.[20]

During these years the standard of living showed clearly a falling tendency from Rs. 49.15 an average of first four years to Rs. 48.8, the average of his subsequent three years. Absolute misery of industrial workers is evident from Table no. 3, which shows that so far as food conditions are concerned prison inmates were better off than the free industrial workers.

Table 2

Per Head Consumption Expenditure

(at 1938-39 Prices)

Year	*Rupees*	*Year*	*Rupees*
1931-32	49.9	1936-37	49.6
1932-33	49.1	1937-38	48.4
1933-34	48.7	1938-39	47.4
1934-35	48.9	1939-40	45.6
1935-36	48.4	1940-41	46.3

Source : Desai, R.C., "Standard of living in India and Pakistan" Bombay, 1953, p. 284.

Table 3

Daily Consumption of Food Per Adult Male

(English Pound)

Food Stuff	*Industrial Worker (Textile Industry)*		*Indian Inmates in the Prison of Bombay with*	
	Bombay	*Madras*	*Light Work*	*Heavy Work*
Cereals	1.29	1.13	1.38	1.50
Pulses	0.09	0.07	0.21	0.27
Meat	0.03	—	0.04	0.04
Salt	0.04	0.05	0.03	0.03
Oils	0.02	0.03	0.03	0.03
Food adjunces	0.07	0.09	—	—
Total	1.54	1.37	1.69	1.87

Source : Kuezynski, Jurgan, Conditions of workers (1980-1950) in Economic History of India 1857-1956, Edited by Singh, V.B., Allied Publishers Pvt. Ltd., New Delhi, 1965, p. 617.

Table 4

Daily Calorie Intake Per Adult Male

Food Stuff	*Industrial Workers (Textile Industry)*		*Indian Inmates in the Prisons of Bombay with*	
	Bombay	*Madras*	*Ligh work*	*Heavy work*
Cereals	2,036	1,774	2,292	2,452
Pulses	174	112	333	427
Meat	16	—	21	21
Salt	—	—	—	—
Oils	81	126	126	126
Food adjuncts	128	164	—	—
Total	2,435	2,176	2,772	3,026

Source: Table No. 3 converted into calories.

It is indeed a poor reflection of Indian Economy that an industrial worker in textile industry of Bombay and Madras could manage to have daily consumption of food estimated at 1.54 and 1.37. British Pound respectively as against 1.69 and 1.87, British Pound authorised for Indian inmates in the prisons of Bombay performing light and heavy work respectively. Similarly calories intake of industrial worker in Bombay and Madras calculated at 2,435 and 2,176 respectively is much less than the calorie intake of Indian prisoners estimated at 2,772 and 3,026 for light and heavy work respectively.

Another proof of growing poverty in India is found in historical records which show that the major industry of the country viz., Agriculture during British rule was stagnant or even deteriorating, threatening to drive down the population below the Malthusian limit of subsistence. The progressive decline in the value of agricultural output per acre, per worker and per head of population as shown in Table No. 5, lends powerful support to the rampant poverty of masses in rural India.

Table 5

Value of Agricultural Output (Rupees)

Period	*Per Acre*			*Per Agricultural Worker*	*Per head of Population*	
	Average	*Food*	*Non-food*		*Total*	*Food*
1900-05	28	26	38	105	26	20
1910-15	27	25	33	97	27	20
1920-25	26	23	36	93	25	18
1930-35	26	23	38	103	25	17
1940-45	26	22	41	103	22	15

Source : Sinha, J.N., "Demographic Trends in Economic History of India, (ed.), Singh, V.B., p. 116.

It is apparent from Table no. 5 that the value of agricultural output per acre, per worker and per head of population declined from Rs. 28 to Rs. 26, Rs. 105 to Rs. 103 and Rs. 26 to Rs. 22 respectively during 1900-1945. Similarly, the value of food grain output per acre and per head of population recorded a fall from Rs. 26 to Rs. 22 and Rs. 20 to Rs. 15 during the same period. These negative trends amply support the contention that poverty was rampant and wide spread in India during British rule.

Dr. Banerjee has aptly summarised the poverty of Indian masses as follows:

"Ill-fed, ill-clad, ill-lodged, the mass of the people of India lead a dull and dreary existence. The want of proper subsistence impairs the vigour and vitality of the

> people, who fall easy victims to the attacks of various kinds of disease. Having no reserve to fall back upon in difficult times, they suffer untold misery, whenever there is a slight distributing cause such as draught or failure of the crops. The children of week and unhealthy parents become weaklings and being themselves ill-fed, and ill-brod, swell the number of the worthless members of society. Thus, the physical deterioration of the people goes on increasing from generation to generation and with the progress of physical degeneration, their moral stamina also tends to become less and less trong".[21]

Many thinkers, while commenting on the economic condition of people during the British Rule have convincingly proved that the policies and programmes had inhabitive effect on development and impoverishment of masses was increasing. Analysing the impact of permanent settlement and freedom of trade, Ram Manohar Roy observed:

> "In so far as these causes had operated to bring about an increase of wealth, it was confined to landlords and dealers in commodities what was too evident was the extent of overwhelming poverty throughout the country (towns and their immediate vicinity excepted)....It is well known that within a circle of a hundred miles in any part of the country, there are to be found very few, if any (besides proprietors of lands) that have the least pretension to wealth or independence, or even the common comforts of life".[22]

He had also come to the conclusion that whatever the system of land tenure—permanent settlement or Ryotwari System—"The condition of the cultivators was very miserable". Under the former they were placed at the mercy of the Zamindar's avaice and ambition and under the latter, they were subjected to the extortion and intrigues of the surveyors and other government revenue officers. G.V. Joshi and Dadabhai Naoroji examined the profile of a dependent and colonial economy of India with a great deal of perception and sophistication and pointed out that poverty in the country was not only deep but also deepening. The exploitative aspect of the Indian economy was vibrantly expressed by Dadabhai Naoroji in his characterisation of the "two Indias"—the two separate worlds that existed in the same country. Dedabhai estimated the percapita income of India at Rs. 20 per annum around the year 1870 and added; "The mass of the people could not get this Rs. 20 as the upper had a larger share than the average also this Rs. 20 per head included the income or produce of foreign planters or producers, in which the interest of the natives did not go further than being mostly common labourers at competitive wages. All the profits of such produce are enjoyed by all carried away from the country by foreigners".[23] It was against this dismal background that Dadabhai spoke of two India's" as follows:

> "In reality there are two Indians—one the prosperous the other poverty stricken. The prosperous India is the India of the British and other foreigners. They exploit India as officials, capitalists in a variety of ways and early away enormous wealth to their country. To them India is, of course, rich and prosperous. The more they can carry away, the richer and more prosperous India is the second India of the Indians—the poverty stricken India".[24]

Romesh Chander Dutt has sought an explanation from the British Rule as to why "the poverty of the Indian people was unparalleled in any civilised country" and why "by a moderate calculation, the famines of 1877, 1878 and 1900 had carried off 15 million people—a population equal to half of England".[25] While discussing the evil economic consequencies of the Age of Imperialism, Dutt mentioned that "It was not gratifying to know that a country possessing a rich and fertile soil, and a feugal and industrious population was still subject to recurring famines after a century and a half of the British rule. There were no signs of increasing prosperity and greater distress—the recurrence of famines was more frequent and desolation caused greater".[26] Inexorable continuity and increasing intensity of India's poverty was indicated by the low per capita income of £ 2 as against £ 48 in Canada and £ 42 in Great Britain".[27]

Foregoing discussions lead to an inevitable conclusion that under British rule India was getting economically unpoverished continuously and therefore, poverty was deepening year after year. Situation on the eve of independence was thus aptly described as, "India was a rich country but inhabited by poor people".

Poverty in the Post-Independence Period

At the time of independence, India was a low income country with a near stagnant economy and a wide-spread poverty inherited from a colonial rule. Since, in a low income country poverty cannot be alleviated without growth, therefore, growth and poverty become concordant. Accordingly during the initial years of development planning, poverty was envisaged to be ameliorated through the spread effects of the various growth oriented programmes and to some extent, through certain special areas and group-based programmes meant for specially less—privileged and depressed sections like Scheduled Castes and Scheduled Tribes with the passage of time it was realised that since the benefits of growth were being shared inequitably, therefore growth by itself was unlikely to reduce the inequality and eliminate poverty. It was an inevitable consequence of a predominantly private resource based economy India as the, better endowed could make a much greater use of the facilities developed in the process of planned development. It was also intriguing to observe that the growth had led to an increase in poverty. Emergence of these trends highlighted the urgency of the programmes aiming not only at accelerated growth but also alleviation of poverty. Hence, around seventies numerous programmes based on area and/or house-hold approach were launched to counter poverty of the broadly indentified groups of poor such as scheduled castes, tribes, small and marginal farmers and landless labourers.

In view of these trends, investigations into as to how the gains of development have been shared among different sections of the society and regions of the country during the post-independence period have centred around inter-personal or size-distribution of income involving two inter-related themes viz.:

(a) Inequality or Relative Poverty

(b) Absolute Poverty

(a) Inequality or Relative Poverty

It refers to the unequal distribution of income and/or expenditure resulting from the unequal earnings of the people which are usually attributed to unequal opportunities unequal abilities, unequal ownership of assets and a host of other institutional factors. Poverty is undoubtedly related to inequality. In the low per capita income countries, high degree of inequality unmistakenly suggests the reality of massive poverty. Common sense tells that a person with income significantly less then a person with income significantly less than the average income of the population is poor. Victor Fuchs has suggested in improved measure of relative poverty by defining poor with incomes less than half of the national median.[28] Obviously, this view cannot be accepted as gospel trouth for relative poverty can be defined as one-third or one-fourth of the median income because basic minimum requirements for a minimum level of living may differ from place to place, from time to time and from group to group. Relative poverty therefore, is time specific, place specific and socio-cultural specific. It must, however, be re-emphasised that though inequality and poverty are not unrealated, neither concept subsumes the other. A transfer of income from the top 20 per cent to next 20 per cent range may reduce inequality but not poverty. A general decline in income may keep degree of inequality unchanged but may lead to a sharp increase in poverty in terms of starvation and malnutrition.

Briefly, role of inequality in the prevalence and perpetuation of poverty should not be under-estimated. Poverty and inequality though, are not conceptually equivalent, inequality does figure prominantly in the analysis of poverty.

The inequality of income and wealth is measured in terms of the percentage of income received or wealth owned by the percentage of people in a country. Amongst several measure of inequality, the following are more prominently used by the researchers :

(a) Gini-co-efficient;

(b) Theil's Index; and

(c) Atkinson's Index.

Gini-co-efficient as a measure of inequality assigns equal weights to the income received by different categories of people. Atkinson's Index gives weights to the income received by different groups of people. Since the weights assigned depend upon the judgement of the researcher therefore, this measure is exposed to the bias of arbitrariness. Theil's Index is useful for comparing inter—as well as intra—group inequalities but its estimation precedure requires more detailed data as compared to other measures. Gini-co-efficient is useful if the Lorenz Curves do not cut each other. Most of the studies conducted in India have adopted Gini-co-efficient as a measure of inequality by estimating the shares of decile groups of population in income and/or wealth in order to improve the reliability of their findings. However, before the findings on income distribution are examined it is necessary to bear in mind the following limitations of the data used by these studies.

1. None of the available data are adequate and up-to-date to afford scientific study of income distribution in India. The data provided by the Central Statistical Organisation (CSO) are hardly useful for the study of the national income distribution. Keeping

in view the fragile and infirm nature of the data, and also the urgency to know the pattern of income distribution, the Government of India in 1960 appointed a committee on Distribution of Income and Levels of Living under the chairmanship of Professor P.C. Mahalanobuto look into whole matter rigorously. The Committee submitted its report in 1964, but since then no similar attempt has been made, therefore comparable information on this issue is not available. Reserve Bank of India, National Council of Applied Economic Reserch and some individual researchers have examined the pattern of income distribution at different points of time with the help of data from different sources and hence, their estimates are incomparable. Professor Pramit Chaudari points out, "Most of the studies take the year 1960-61 as a bench mark year for purposes of comparison. The most recent data to which comparisons can be made relate to the late 1960's, e.g. 1968-69. This is an important point, for their is evidence in the form of an acceleration in the rate of inflation, a faltering in the growth of agricultural production and continuing industrial stagnation that matters have grown worse for the poor and the lower-paid since the late 1960's. Whatever our conclusions are regarding the state of the poor in India, they are likely to be an understatement of the problem, on the basis of the available data".[29]

2. Most of the studies on the size distribution of income are based on the derivation of incomes from the consumption expenditure data collected by National Sample Survey. The underlying assumption in this case is that the degree of inequality in income distribution would be the same as in case of the pattern of consumption expenditure among different categories. This assumption does not appear to be realistic, for degree of inequality in consump-

tion expenditure is smaller than for incomes.[30] While no satisfactory explanation for this discrepancy is offered, it is attributed partly to the poor man's access to non-marked forces at (nearly) zero prices such as forest product, game etc. or pently to the fact that richer housedolds save a larger than the average fraction of their incomes, whereas the poor ones, as a group, are net dis-savers.

Further, the estimates of aggregate consumption derived from the NSS data for particular years e.g., 1967-68 are 10 per cent below the consumption estimates made from the national income statistics.[31] This indicates that either of these must be an under- or over estimate of the actual consumption. Srinivasan and others have argued that the discrepancies are greater for point estimates than over a period of time but that each is subject to error.[32] Also, different studies e.g., the NSS and NCAER surveys, conducted roughly for the same period, give slightly different figures for the size distribution of consumption expenditure.[33]

3. Normally, income or consumption expenditure data are available at current prices and needs to be deflated to obtain real values in order to make inter-temporal or spatial comparisons. Differences in the consumption patterns of various groups and also price variations of the identical goods cause problems involved in the choice of a corrent price deflator for purposes of comparisons, either on an all-India basis or between states.

4. Owing to these deficiencies in data, it is necessary to use some conversion factors in order to build a complete picture from fragmented data. Accordingly Dandekar and Rath assume that top 30 per cent of the population would have faced no worse interms of consumption between 1960-61 and 1967-68 than at

lower group.[34] Similarly, with the view to estimate total expenditure from expenditure on food, Bardhan uses a conversion factors appropriate to the bottom 30 per cent, no more and no less, of the population.[35]

5. Almost all studies have used income-tax data along with NSS data to estimate income distribution pattern. In India, around one per cent people pay income tax. agricultural incomes are exempted from tax and there. is widespread tax evasion therefore, data obtained from income tex records are both inadequate and unsatisfactory for estimating the pattern of income distribution.

These aberrations apart, estimates of inequality of incomes/consumption expenditures have been attempted by various researchers at different points of time. Even though these estimates are incomparable, it is worthwhile to present them in the following pages, for they do reflect broadly the pattern of income distribution at a specific point of time.

1. Lydall's Estimates of Income Distribution

In one of his pioneering studies, F.H. Lydall calculated the income distribution pattern for the year 1955-56 by utilising the data obtained from income-tax records and the NSS data on consumption expenditure.[36] His findings reveal that per capita income of 86 per cent of the households was less than 360 (at current prices) per annum and of these, 69 per cent had an annual per capita income of Rs. 240 (at current prices) or less. He also pointed out that per capita income of about 72 per cent people was less than the national average of 255 (at current prices) and the remaining 28 per cent people concerned 51 per cent of the national income while the poorest 25 per cent of the population accounted for only 9.5 per eent of the national income. He also noted that top 10 per cent households had garnered 34 per cent of country's national income.

2. Estimates of Iyengar and Mukherjee

N.S. Iyengar and M.M. Mukherjee jointly worked out the distribution of personal household income for the years 1952-53, 1953-54 and 1956-57.[37] They did not consider the use of income tax data appropriate to estimate personal income distribution and therefore, adopted NSS data pertaining to the size distribution of total consumer expenditure and aggregate saving estimates calculated by the Reserve Bank of India for their analysis. Their Chief findings are summarised in Table No. 6.

It is clear from Table No. 6 that top 5 per cent of the househeld recorded an increase in the share of personal income from 14 per cent in 1952-53 to 17.5 per cent in 1956-75. Likewise the shares of top 10 per cent and bottom 20 per cent rose from 24 per cent to 25 per cent and from 7.5 per cent to 8.5 per cent respectively during the corresponding period. It is thus obvious that improvement in the shares of these fractile groups was at the cost of middle income graup.

Table 6

Estimates of Personal Income Distribution

Fractile Group (P.C. of Household	*Iyengar and Mukherjees Estimates*		
	1952-53	*1953-54*	*1954-55*
95—100	14.0	14.0	17.5
90—100	24.0	23.0	25.0
0— 20	7.5	8.0	8.5

Source: Iyengar and Mukherjee, (1961).

3. Estimates of the Reserve Bank of India

The study of the Reserve Bank of India on Income distribution covered a three year period from 1953-54 to 1956-57.[38]

It was based on all the available data but did not use the absolute magnitudes of the NSS data and Income Tax data, instead it applied the proportions revealed in these data to the households and incomes independently. The study did not use NSS data for a single year rather, it used two year averages beginning from 1953-54. The main conclusions of the study are presented in the Table No. 7.

Table 7

Estimate of the Income Distribution

(R.B.I. Study)

Fractile Group of P.C. of Household	*Rural*	*Urban*	*Total*
95—100	17	26	20
90—100	25	37	28
50— 90	44	38	44
0— 20	9	7	8

Source: R.B.I. 'Distribution of Income in the Indian Economy, 1953-54 to 1956-57. Reserve Bank of India, September, 1962.

Table No. 7 reveals that the top 5 per cent of the households commanded a share of 20 per cent in the national income while as their share was 17 per cent and 26 per cent in rural and urban areas respectively. It also shows that the bottom 20 per cent of the households accounted for 8 per cent of the national income as against 9 per cent and 7 per cent in the rural and urban sectors respectively. Thus, the study revealed that income distribution was more skewed in the urban than in the rural sector.

4. Estimates of National Council of Applied Economic Research

The National Council of Applied Economic Research analysed the problem of income distribution without using the

NSS and income tax data. Rather, it independently carried out an urban household survey of income and saving in 1960 and a rural household survey of income and savings in 1962. Later it conducted another All India Consumer Expenditure Survey in 1964-65. The results of these surveys[39] are summarised in Tables 8 & 9.

Table 8

Estimates of Income Distribution (1960) NCAER

Fractile Group P.C. of Household	*Rural*	*Urban*
Top 5 per cent	–	31.0
Top 10 per cent	33.6	42.4
Top 50 per cent	79.3	83.0
Bottom 20 per cent	4.0	4.0

Source: NCAER, Urban Income and Saving (New Delhi, 1962), Quoted in the Report of the Committee (Mahalnobis Committee) on Distribution of Income and Levels of Living, p. 14.

It is seen from Table No. 8 that top 10 per cent of households sector garnered 42.4 per cent of aggregate income in urban sector as against 33.6 per cent of rural income concerned by their counterpart in the rural sector. Top 50 per cent urban households enjoyed 83 per cent of urban income in contrast to 79.3 per cent of rural income by their counterparts in the rural sector. However, bottom 20 per cent households accounted for only 4 per cent of the respective incomes in rural and urban sectors. These observations clearly reveal that income inequality in the urban is more pronounced than in the rural areas.

It stems from the table No. 9 that personal income distribution by decile groups or population is less skewed than by the decile groups of households; approximately 47.5 per cent of

Table 9

Percentage Distribution of Disposable Personal Income by Decile Groups of Population and Households (NCAER, 1964-65)

Decile Groups of Population from Bottom (Percentages)	*% Share in Total Income*	*Decile Groups of of Households from Bottom (Percentage)*	*Rural Sector % Share in Total Income*	*Urban Sector % Share in Total Income*	*Total % Share in Total Income*
1	*2*	*3*	*4*	*5*	*6*
0—10	3.14	0—10	3.00	2.26	2.68
10—20	4.36	10—20	4.38	3.26	3.23
20—30	5.13	20—30	5.39	4.13	4.88
30—40	5.99	30—40	6.40	4.83	5.83
40—50	6.85	40—50	7.42	5.83	6.72
50—60	7.72	50—60	8.34	7.02	7.65
60—70	8.81	60—70	9.56	8.71	8.75
70—80	10.51	70—80	10.85	9.97	10.37

1		*2*	*3*		*4*	*5*	*6*
80— 90		14.14	80— 90		13.75	14.11	14.09
90—100		33.35	90—100		30.90	39.88	35.11
Bottom	20%	7.50	Bottom	20%	7.39	5.52	6.60
Top	20%	47.49	Top	20%	44.65	53.95	49.20
Lorenz Ratio		0.39	Larenz Ratio		0.35	0.46	0.41

Source: The NCAER, All India Consumer Expenditure Survey, Vol. I & II, (New Delhi, 1966-67).

the disposable income has gone to top 20 per sent and about 7.5 per cent to the bottom 20 per cent of the population as against 49.2 per cent and 5.91 per cent to the top 20 per cent and bottom 20 per cent of the household respectively. The Lorenz ratio of 0.39 for the population is less than for the households estimated at 0.41. This Table also shows that there is more unequal distribution of disposable income in urban sector with Lorenz ratio of 0.46 than the rural section having a Lorenz ratio of 0.35.

5. Estimates of Ojha and Bhatt

P.D. Ojha and V.V. Bhatt have in their joint study estimated the income distribution in India for two years; 1963-64 and 1964-65 by utilising the CSO data on national income, estimates of direct taxes paid by unincorporated business and household saving data.[40] Data derived from these sources have been used to estimate the aggregate consumption expenditure which is distributed among the decile expenditure groups of population on the basis of relevant NSS percentage distribution. Savings have been added to the consumption expenditure of the top-most group on the assumption that they are made only by the richest and this aggregate is taken as income (Y=C+S) of the group. For all other groups, income is taken equivalent to their consumption expenditure (Y=C). This methodology tends to underestimate the degree of inequality, for it ignores net dissaving of the lower expenditure groups. The main results of the study are tabulated below on page next.

The nature of income inequality is quite obvious from Table no. 10 as top 20 per cent of population accounts for 48 per cent of disposable personal income and the share of bottom 20 per cent of population is only 7 per cent. The high degree of inequality is also evident from the Lorenz ratio of 0.375.

Table 10

Percentage Distribution of Disposable Personal Income 1963-64 & 1964-65

Decile Groups of Population from Bottom Percentage	*Average of 1963-64 & 1964-65*
0— 10	3
10— 20	4
20— 30	5
30— 40	6
40— 50	6
50— 60	7
60— 70	9
70— 80	12
80— 90	13
90—100	36
Bottom 20%	7
Top 10%	48
Lorenz Ratio	0.375

Source: T.N. Srinivasan and P.K. Bardhan, Poverty and Income Distribution in India, Calcutta, 1974, p. 104.

6. Estimates of Ranadive

K.R. Ranadive in her estimates of income distribution for 1961-62 taxes care of the tax evasion by the rich and the net dissaving of the poor.[41] She makes two alternative estimates on the basis of two sets of assumption.

(i) that urban households with income less than Rs. 2000

and rural households with income less than Rs. 720 have zero net savings and all evaded tax payments are fully reflected in consumption and/or savings.

(ii) that urban households with income less than Rs. 3000 and rural households with income less than Rs. 1200 are assumed to have net dissavings. The net dissavings of the urban households in lower income bracket are assumed to be 25 per cent of the total urban savings, whereas far poor rural households are assumed to be 14 per cent of the total rural savings. The evasions are assumed not to be reflected in consumption and/or savings.

As a consequence, estimates based on second assumption show a greater degree of inequality than the estimates built around first assumption as 13 seen in Table No. 11. (next page).

Data in the Table No. 11 vividly reveals that income inequality under the second assumption with an estimated Lorenz ratio of 0.67 is higher than under the first assumption with the Lorenz ratio calculated at 0.351.

7. Madalgi's Estimates of Personal Income Distribution

S.S. Madalgi estimated personal income distribution for the year 1971 and arrived at the conclusion that personal income distribution is relatively more unequally distributed in the urban than in the rural areas.[42] His findings are summarized in the Table No. 12.

It is evident from the Table No. 12 that the ratio of per capita income in the lowest to the highest expenditure class is higher (1:12.8) in urban than in the rural areas (1:8.7). Further, 8 per cent of the urban population in the expenditure class of Rs. 55 and above enjoys 40.1 per cent of disposable income as against 2.8 per cent of population enjoying 13.6 per cent disposable income in the rural areas. It is thus obvious that there is affluence of the few and poverty of the mass of population.

Table 11

Percentage Distribution of Disposable Personal Income

K R. Ranadive (1961-62)

Decile Groups of Population from Bottom Percentage	*Ranadive 1961-62*	
	Assumption I	*Assumption II*
0— 10	3.40	3.29
10— 20	4.40	4.31
20— 30	5.39	5.21
30— 40	6.25	5.97
40— 50	7.06	6.70
50— 60	8.16	8.06
60— 70	9.18	8.86
70— 80	10.69	10.90
80— 90	16.37	15.81
90—100	29.10	30.89
Bottom 20	7.80	7.60
Top 20	54.47	46.70
Lorenz Ratio	0.351	0.367

Source: T.N. Srinivasan and P.K. Bardhan, Poverty and Income Distribution in India, (Calcutta, 1974), p. 104.

Briefly, all these studies suggest that during the period under review, income inequalities in the country were quite pronounced, however, distribution of income in the rural areas was less skewed than in the urban areas. Tendulkar for this analysis of the pattern of income distribution divided the planned development period into two phases, viz., sustained growth phase or Phase I covering a period of first three five year Plans (1950-51 to 1964-65) and declaration phase or Phase II

Table 12

Personal Income Distribution in India in 1971-72

At 1960-61 Prices

Monthly Expenditure Class (in Rs.)	*Per Capita Annual Income (in Rs.)*		*Disposable Income as % of Total Income*		*Population in Expenditure Class as % of Total Population*	
	Rural	*Urban*	*Rural*	*Urban*	*Rural*	*Urban*
0—18	187	168	30.8	13.1	54.0	35.1
18—21	299	251	10.5	6.5	11.5	11.8
21—28	363	313	17.1	12.8	15.5	18.6
28—34	477	400	1.6	8.5	7.9	9.8
34—43	577	487	10.1	9.4	5.4	8.9
43—55	731	616	6.3	9.6	2.9	7.2
55 & above	1636	2149	13.6	40.1	2.8	8.6

Source: Compiled from S.S. Madalgi, Population and Food Survey in India, p. 81.

covering a period from 1964-65 to 1973-74 and made the following observations.[43]

> "The Gini co-efficient for the rural population decreased whereas that for the urban population increased during the sustained growth phase. The structure of the size distribution of personal (pre-tax) household incomes at current prices did not change at the all-India level between 1953-54 to 1964-65. The declaration phase, since the mid-sixties is marked by a movement in the opposite direction. The Gini co-efficient for the rural sector recorded an increase and that for the urban sector a decline between 1964-65 and 1975-76 with all-India co-efficient showing no signs of change".

Partial support to these observations has been lent by the findings of an All-India Household Survey conducted by NCAER in 1972,[44] the results of which are presented in the Table No. 13.

Table 13

Percentage Share of Household Disposable Income in Aggregate Income for Different Fractile Groups

Fractile Group	*Percentage Share in Disposable Income*				
	1962		*1967-68*		*All-India*
	Urban	*Rural*	*Urban*	*Rural*	
0— 10	1.3	2.1	2.0	1.8	1.8
10— 20	2.8	3.8	3.2	3.2	3.0
20— 30	3.7	4.7	4.3	3.8	3.7
30— 40	4.7	5 6	4.9	4.5	4.6
40— 50	6.6	6.3	6.1	5.7	5.8
50— 60	6 7	8.2	7.3	7.1	7.0
60— 70	8.3	9.5	8.9	8.8	9.0
70—80	10.7	11.7	10.0	11.8	11.8
80— 90	15.8	15.3	15.6	17.3	16 9
90—100	40.4	32.8	36.9	36.1	36.5
Lorenz Co-efficiency of Concentration	0.49	0.41	0.46	0.46	0.46

Source: NCAER, All India Household Survey of Income, Savings and Consumer Expenditure, December 1971, p. 26.

Analysis of Table No. 13 indicates that share of the bottom 20 per cent households in the disposable income has declined from 5.9 per cent in 1962 to 5.0 per cent in 1967-68 while as the share of top 20 per cent households recorded a rise from 48.1 per cent to 53.4 per cent during the same period.

This suggests a tendency towards increasing concentratin in the rural household sector. In the urban sector, bottom 20 per cent households accounted for 5.2 per cent of disposable income in 1967-68 as against 4.1 per cent in 1962 whereas the share of top 20 per cent of the households decreased from 56.2 per cent in 1962 to 52.5 per cent in 1967-68. This indicates a trends towards decline in the degree of inequality in the urban areas. The rise in the Lorenz Co-efficient of concentration for rural areas from 0.41 in 1962 to 0.46 in 1967-68 and decline for urban areas from 0.49 in 1962 to 0.46 in 1967-68 substantiate the above conclusion.

Trends in Consumer Expenditure

Study of the differentials in the levels of living is better concerned with the help of the analysis of size distribution of the consumer expenditure because the levels of living tend to a fairly stable and their range of variation across different sections of the population is limited. Also because a fairly comparable series for the size distribution of per capita expenditure (at current prices) is available from the National Sample Survey Organisation Dandekar and Rath made a pioneering study of the NSS data on the consumer expenditure for the period 1960-61 and 1967-68[45] results of which are presented in the Table No. 14.

Information provided by this Table reveals that all sections of rural population recorded an increase in the per capita expenditure from 1960-61, to 1967-68, excepting the bottom 5 per cent in whose case it remained stable at Rs. 75. However, in the urban areas per capital expenditure of the bottom 50 per cent population showed a decllne while as the top 50 per cent population experienced an increase during the same period. This indicates an improvement in the levels of living in the rural areas as against worsening of the situation for the bottom 50 per cent of the urban population. However, wide disparity in the per capita expenditure of the bottom and top sections of population in both the rural and urban areas is quite apparent suggesting that the gains of development have been appropria-

Table 14

Per Capita Annual Consumer Expenditure in Different Sections of Rural and Urban Population in 1960-61 and 1967-68 (1960-61 Prices)

Section of Population	*Rural* 1960-61 (*Rs.*)	*Rural* 1967-68 (*Rs.*)	*Urban* 1960-61 (*Rs.*)	*Urban* 1967-68 (*Rs.*)
0— 5	75	75	96	78
5— 10	100	102	130	112
10— 20	124	127	156	146
20— 30	150	153	191	183
30— 40	174	179	224	220
40— 50	198	205	257	256
50— 60	227	206	297	304
60— 70	259	270	343	359
70— 80	303	316	421	442
80— 90	382	399	554	580
90— 95	493	515	753	790
95—100	871	909	1269	1230
All Sections	259	209	356	364

Source: V.M. Dandekar and N. Rath, Poverty in India.

ted by the richer classes and the living standards of the lower income groups have either remained stationary or have positively deteriorated.

An identical conclusion is arrived at by the Planning Commission,[46] Government of India from its estimates of distribution of consumption expenditure on the basis of 32nd Round of National Sample Survey as is evident from Table No. 15.

Table 15

Distribution of Total Private Consumption Expenditure by Deciles, 1977-78

Decile	*Rural (%)*	*Urban (%)*
0— 10	3.7	3.4
10— 20	5.1	4.7
20— 30	6.2	5.6
30— 40	6.6	6.5
40— 50	8.0	7.4
50— 60	8.7	8.7
60— 70	9.8	9.8
70— 80	11.8	12.3
80— 90	14.5	14.2
90—100	25.6	27.4
0—100	100.00	120.0

Source: The Sixth Plan (1980-85).

It is observed from the Table No. 15 that in the rural areas bottom 20 per cent of the population accounts for 8.8 per cent of total private consumption expenditure as against 40.1 per cent enjoyed by the top 20 per cent of the population. In the urban areas, share of the bottom 20 per cent population in the total private consumption cxpenditure is estimated at 8.1 per cent while as the share of top 20 per cent population is calculated at 41.6 per cent. These observations suggested their private consumption expenditure is highly unevenly distributed in both the rural as well as the urban areas.

Tendulkar has compiled from different sources the Gini Co-efficients,[47] calculated on the basis of NSS data and the same are presented in Table No. 16.

Table 16

Gini Co-efficient of the Size Distribution of Normal per Capita Household Private Consumption Expenditure

Sr. No.	*Year*	*Rural*	*India*	*Urban*	*India*
1.	1953-54	0.334		0.381	
2.	1954-55	3.350		0.390	
3.	1955-56	0.344		0.368	
4.	1956-57	0.332		0.394	
5.	1957-58	0.344		0.359	
6.	1958-59	0.340		0.348	
7.	1959-60	0.314		0.357	
8.	1960-61	0.321	0.321	0.350	0.348
9.	1961-62	0.312	0.313	0.357	0 357
10.	1962-63	NA	NA	NA	NA
11.	1963-64	0.297	0.297	0.360	0.360
12.	1964-65	0.294	0 294	0.349	0.349
13.	1965-66	NA	0.297	NA	0.339
14.	1966-67	NA	0.293	NA	0 337
15.	1967-68	0.293	0.291	0.345	0.332
16.	1968-69		0.305		0.329
17.	1969-70		0.293		0.340
18.	1970-71		0.283		0.327
19.	1971-72	NA	NA	NA	NA
20.	1972-73		0.299		0.341
21.	1973-74		0.276		0.301
22.	1974-75				
23.	1975-76				
24.	1976-77				
25.	1977-78		0.336		0.344
26.	1983		0.297		0.325

Source: Columns (2) and (4) from G.S. Chatterjee and N. Bhattacharya, "On Disparities in Per Capita Household Consumption in India". In T.N. Srinivasan and P.K. Bardhan (eds.), Poverty and Income Distribution in India, Statistical Publishing Society, Calcutta, 1974.

Columns (3) and (5) from S.P. Gupta and K.L. Datta, "Poverty Calculations in the Sixth Plan," Economic and Political Weekly, April 14, 1984.

It appears from the table No. 16 that the Gini Co-efficients for the rural population declined slightly from 0.33 in 1953-54 to 0.32 in 1960-61 and further to 0.293 in 1967-68, Gini Co-efficient for the urban population is also seen to have declined from 0.39 in the mid 1950's to 0.35 by 1960 61, followed by a rise to 0.36 in 1963-64 and a decline to 0.345 in 1967-68.

Tendulkar poses a question as to whatever the observed reduction in the inequality is a purely monetary illusion (because of changing prices over time) or whether it could be taken to hold in real terms as well. He attempted an answer on the basis of the relative price movements for different decile groups of population and concluded that the greater reduction in the urban Gini Co-efficient than the rural one from 1953-54 to 1960-61 may be expected to hold in real terms. However, during the four years (1960-61 to 1964-65) the reduction observed for the rural population would overstate the reduction in real terms. Whereas for the urban population, there may have been a worsening of relative inequality because of the regressive nature of the price rise. The continuation of the regressive price rise during the later years may be expected to result in the decline in Gini Co-efficient over-stating the reduction in the relative inequality in real terms for the urban population. A slight reduction recorded in nominal terms for the rural population could possibly reflect worsening or unchanged relative inequality in real terms when compared to 1954-65.[48] Foregoing discussion inevitably suggests that the relative inequality in levels of living in real terms has been lower towards the mid-1970's than in the early 1950's. It is further seen that the Gini-coefficient rose in 1977-78 and fell again in 1983.

Iyengar and Brahamnada estimated the Gini-Lorenz Ratio on the basis of the various rounds of NSS data to analyse the movements in the consumer expenditure pattern in rural and urban areas.[49] Their estimates of Gini-Lorenz Ratio are presented in Tables 17 & 18.

Table 17

Lorenz Ratio

Year	*Round*	*Rural*	*Urban*
1952	4th	0.340	0 365
1953-53	5th	0.330	0.397
1953-54	7th	0.334	0.371
1954-55	8th	0.350	0.370
1955	9th	0.335	0.371
1955-56	10th	0 344	0.368
1956 57	11th	0.319	0.402
1957	12th	0.331	0.393
1957-58	13th	0.333	0.377
1958-59	14th	0.328	0.348
1959-60	15th	0.314	0.357
1960-61	16th	0.321	0.350
1961-62	17th	0.316	0.362
1962-64	18th	0.300	0.366
1964-65	19th	0.297	0.357
1965-66	20th	0.301	0.347
1966-67	21st	0.298	0.349
1967-68	22nd	0.296	0.348
1968-69	23rd	0.310	0.346
1969-70	24th	2.298	0.362
1970-71	25th	0.289	0.352
1972-73	26th	0.304	0.348
1973-74	28th	0.282	0.310
1977-78	32nd	0.340	0.352
1983	38th	0.296	0.332

Source: NSS Data.

Table 18

Plan-wise Average Gini-Lorenz Ratio

Plan	*Number of Observations*	*Rural*	*Urban*
I (1951-1956)	6	0.34	0.38
II (1956-1960)	6	0.33	0.37
III (1961-1965)	4	0.30	0.35
(1961-1968)	3	0.30	0.33
IV (1969-1973)	4	0.29	0.33
V (1974-1979)	1	0.31	0.33
(1979-1980)*	NA	NA	NA
VI (1980-1984)	1	0.30	0.33

* Annual Plans.

Analysis of the information contained in Table No. 17 and 18 reveals that inequality in the consumer expenditure pattern was higher during the 1950's than in the subsequent decades, for observed Gini-Lorenz Ratio is consistently declining in both the rural as well as urban areas from 0.34 and 0.38 respectively during 1951-56 to 0.29 to 0.33 during 1969-73. However, the Gini-Lorenz Ratio for the rural areas rose to 0.31 during 1974-79 but fell again to 0.30 during 1980-84, whereas for the urban areas it remained stable at 0.33 during all these years. It is also obvious that the distribution in the rural areas has tended to become stable from the early sixties while as far urban areas stability is observed from the late sixties onwards. Another noticeable observation is that the Gini-Lorenz Ratio for the urban areas is higher than the rural areas during the entire period, suggesting that inequality is more pronounced in the former than in the latter areas. These conclusions are further supported by the analysis of the relative percentage shares of the bottom half of the population

(Q0.5) in the consumption expenditure for the period 1952 and 1983 as contained in the Table No. 19.

Table 19

The Relative Percentage Share of Bottom Half of Population (Q0.5) in Consumption Expenditure

Year	*Share of Bottom Half*	
	Rural	*Urban*
1952	27.41	25.23
1952-53	27.75	23.55
1953-54	27.53	24 91
1954-55	25.98	24.04
1955-56	26.84	25 14
1957	28.12	25.02
1957-58	27.81	26.04
1959-60	29.94	26.82
1960-61	28.40	26.39
1961-62	29.07	25.87
1963-64	30.14	26.18
1964-65	30.38	26.71
1965-66	30.00	27.3
1966-67	30.9	27.4
1967-68	30.2	27.4
1968-69	29.5	27.6
1969-70	30.3	27.0
1970-71	30.9	27.4
1972-73	30.4	27.6
1973-74	31.4	29.8
1977-78	29.6	27.5
1983	30.0	28.1

Source: NSS Rounds.

Perusal of the information given in the Table No. 19 reveals that the relative percentage share of the bottom half of population in consumption expenditure is higher in rural than in the urban areas for the entire period from 1952 to 1983, thus showing lesser degree of inequality in rural than in urban areas. The data also shows an improvement in the levels of living in both rural as well as urban areas, for relative shares in these areas have moved upward.

Some other studies such as those of Iyengar and Bhattacharya[50] and Vaidyanathan[51] pointed out that price unadjusted consumption distribution do not reveal the underlying trends in real consumption distribution since price movements have differential impacts on different segments of the distribution. Iyengar and Jain observed that the decile wise price movements are of the type that the poorer sections were affected by inflation more severely than the rich during the period 1963-64 to 1973-74.[52] Radhakrishna and Sharma estimated that the inequalities in the living levels, after adjustment for prices started widening during the period beginning from 1963-64.[53] Iyengar and Suryanarayana estimated the per capita consumption and Lorenz Ratio's based on current price distributions separately for the rural and urban sectors of India for the period 1961-62 to 1973-74.[54] The findings of the study are summed up in Table No. 20.

Table 20

Estimates of Per Capita Consumption and Lorenz Ratio based on Current Price Distribution—India (Rural and Urban), 1961-62 to 1973-74

	Per Capita Consumption (Rs. per month)		*Lorenz Ratio*	
Year	*Rural*	*Urban*	*Rural*	*Urban*
1961-62	21.73	30.86	0.3130	0.3566
1963-64	22.37	32.96	0.2974	0.3596
1964-65	26.44	36.03	0.2936	0.3492
1965-66	30.90	41.54	0.2934	0.3368
1967-68	33.40	44.82	0.2908	0.3324
1968-69	33.29	46.04	0.3051	0.3292
1969-70	34.70	50.34	0.2928	0.3403
1970-71	35.31	52.85	0.2831	0.3265
1972-73	44.17	63.33	0.2993	0.3410
1973-74	53.01	70.77	0.2758	0.3013

Source: Suryanarayan, (1980).

Perusal of the data given in Table No. 20 shows a perceptible increase in the per capita consumption expenditure and also an improvement in the distribution as is indicated by a decline in the Lorenz Ratio's for both the rural and urban sectors during the period under study. This may suggest a marked increase in aggregate welfare in the rural and urban sectors of India. However, estimates made by them on the basis of deflated distribution show that the movements in the real magnitudes are different from those revealed by the price unadjusted estimates as is seen from Table No. 21.

Table 21

Estimate of Per Capita Consumption and Lorenz Ratio (at 1961-62 Prices)—India (Rural and Urban), 1961-62 to 1973-74

	Per Capita Consumption (Rs. per month)		*Lorenz Ratio*	
Year	*Rural*	*Urban*	*Rural*	*Urban*
1961-62	21.73	30.86	0.3100	0.3560
1963-64	20.31	30.24	0.3000	0.3630
1964-65	20.88	29.51	0.3080	0 3640
1965-66	20.84	27.90	0.3090	0.3540
1966-67	19.78	27.94	0.3120	0.3620
1967-68	18.80	27.19	0.3150	0.3650
1968-69	19.49	28 58	0.3260	0 3550
1969-70	19 45	29.75	0.3140	0.3640
1970-71	19.30	30.14	0.3010	0.3490
1972-73	20 58	32.96	0.3220	0.3710
1973-74	21 51	30.60	0 2990	0.3460

Source: Suryanarayan, (1980)

It is observed from Table No. 21 that the per capita consumption did not indicate any significant trend is either of the two sectors. It fell in the early part of the period and rose more or less steadily from around 1967-68 onwards, in both the sectors. The Lorenz Ratio's also did not show any consistent trend. They fluctuated around a stagnant trend in both rural and urban sectors. On the basis of these findings they concluded that consumption and inequality levels remained stagnant in the two sectors during 1961-62 to 1973-74.

On the basis of foregoing discussion, following broad conclusions are arrived at :

(i) Inequality is more pronounced in the pattern of income distribution than in the distribution of consumer expenditure.

(ii) Degree of inequality in income as well as expenditure is higher in urban than in the rural areas of India.

(iii) Inequality in the distribution of income and expenditure in both the rural and urban sectors has declined at current prices while as at constant prices no firm trend is evident.

B. Incidence of Absolute Poverty

Generally, measurement of the prevalence of poverty is attempted with the help of two approaches viz., direct approach and income approach. According to the 'direct' approach, minimum levels of one or a combination of essential basic needs are specified and the incidence of poverty is measured in terms of the proportion of the population that falls below these levels. In the 'income' approach poverty is measured in terms of the proportion of the population with less than the minimum income needed to acquire some basic bundles of goods and services. This is not to say that the two are not linked. On the basis of these two approaches, numerous studies have been made from time to time by experts including the Planning Commission to evaluate the extent and dimensions of poverty in India. In most of the studies, incidence of poverty has been measured in terms of the percentage of the total population below a normatively specified poverty line reflecting basically some 'low enough' yet 'reasonable' minimum level of living Besides controversies centering around the elements of subjectivity in the 'low enough' and 'reasonable' concepts, data deficiencies and unresolved methodological issues have made it extremely difficult to obtain a comprehensive picture of poverty in India. Despite these lacunae, estimates relating to the incidence of poverty made by various experts including Planning Commission are helpful in understanding the nature and extent of poverty in the country. Accordingly main points of some of the studies made on the incidence of povorty in India are summarized in the subsequent pages to comprehend magnitude of the problem.

In 1962, Government of India appointed a study group comprising Prof. D.R. Gadgil, B.N. Ganguli, P.S. Lokanathan, M.R. Masani, Ashok Mehta, Shriman Narayan Pitamber Pant, V.K.R.V. Rao and Anna Saheb Saharasbudhe which recommended a standard private consumption of Rs. 20 per capita per month as demarcating the poverty line. The group excluded expenses on medical and educational facilities from the total computed expenditure on the assumption that these shall be distributed cost-free by the state in accordance with its constitutional obligations. These recommendations of the group are criticised on the basis that 'a per capita per month expenditure of Rs. 20 without a reference to the prices of a number of essential commodities does not make clear the implied level of living sufficiently explicit. Further, it does not make any distinction between rural and urban living costs.

P.O. Ojha (1970)[55] in one of his studies estimates both rural and urban poverty for 1960-61 and rural poverty for 1967-68 by using diet intake of 2250 calories per capita per day and NSS data on personal expenditure. He assumes that 66 per cent of this calorie intake must be obtained from grains, cereals and pulses in urban areas while as the corresponding figure for rural areas was 80 per cent. On the basis of these assumptions he works out the food requirement at 518 g and 432 g per day per person in rural and urban areas respective y. By adopting NSS data, he reaches the conclusion that in rural areas (1960-61) for per capita expenditure range from 0.00 to Rs. 15-18, there existed deficiencies in food grain consumption in relation to minimum calorie requirements. For the urban population, nutritional deficiency persisted for individuals in two expenditure groups i.e., from Rs. 0-8 and Rs. 8-11 per month. From these findings, he concludes that the demarcation line between the poor and non-poor should be Rs. 18 per month in the rural areas and Rs. 11 in the urban areas. On this basis, he estimates that in 1960-61, approximately 51.8% of the rural population as 184.2 million people and 7.6 per cent or 6 million people in urban areas lived in poverty. He also concluded that in 1967-68, 70 per cent of the rural population was below the minimum level of food-grains consumption.

Ojha's study suffers from certain drawbacks. It has not included the expenditure on health, education and housing while estimating the poverty line. The study has adopted the uniform minimum nutritional requirements i.e., 2,250 calories per person per day for the rural and urban population despite differences in socio-economic and cultural environment which in turn cause the difference in the calorie intake requirements in these settings. Further, price differentials in the two areas have also been ignored while calculating the poverty line.

Following the recommendation of the study group, B.S. Minhas (1970)[56] adopts the figure of Rs. 240 per person per annum as a poverty line for the urban areas, however, for

Table 22

Percentage and Number of People below Minimum Levels of Living

Year	*Below Rs. 240 per annum*		*Below Rs 200 per annum*	
	% age	*Million*	*% age*	*Million*
1956-67	65.0	215	52.4	173
1957-58	63.2	212	50.4	169
1960-61	59.4	211	46.0	164
1961-62	56.4	206	43 6	159
1963 64	57.8	221	44.2	169
1964-65	51 6	200	39.2	154
1967-68	50.6	210	37.1	154

Source: B.S. Minhas, (1970).

rural population a low figure of Rs. 200 is considered appropriate by him on the ground that rural cost of living trends to be lower at 1960-61 prices. On the basis of both the figures, he estimates the extent of poverty in the rural areas, the findings are summarised in the Table No. 22.

It is observed from Table No. 22 that the number of people below the poverty line of Rs. 200 decreased from 193 million in 1956-57 to 154 million in 1967-68 i.e., from 52.6 per cent of rural population to 37.1 per cent in the respective years. It is also seen that number of people below the poverty line of Rs. 240 decreased marginally from 215 million to 210 million while as the percentage decline from 65.0 to 50.6 was significant. This decline is largely explained by the growth in the average per capita consumption in real terms rather than by the slight fall in the concentration index of consumer expenditure. He further concludes that the number of poor tend to rise in bad harvest years.

Bardhan (1970)[57] questions the validity of the GNP deflator as used by Minhas on the ground that is covers both agricultural and manufactured commodities and as such has a tendency to understate the rise in prices paid by the rural poor because his budget includes a much smaller proportion of the manufacturers than the national average. Instead, he adopts the official agricultural labour consumer price index for deflating the consumption of the rural poor and the working class consumer price index for deflating the consumption of the urban poor. Like many other researchers, he relies on the NSS data on consumption expenditure. Thus, he draws the poverty line for rural sector at Rs. 15 and for urban sector at Rs. 18 at 1960-61 prices on the ground that the rural prices are generally lower than the urban prices. Accordingly, he estimates 135 million persons constituting 38 per cent of rural population as rural poor and 34 million people comprising 44 per cent of the urban population as urban poor in 1960-61. Using the same norms both for rural and urban areas, he suggests that at 1960-61 prices in 1968-69 as many as 54 per cent of the rural population and 41 per cent of the urban population were poor.

One of the major objections against the methodology adopted by Bardhan particularly regarding the uses of agricultural labour consumer price index for deflating the consumption of the rural poor is that small farmers is very large numbers are also included in the category of rural poor and their consumption pattern is not necessarily the same as that of agricultural labourers. Secondly, the appropriateness of the price imputed for consumption of self-produced agricultural commodities is also questionable. Lastly, Bardhan uses Rs. 15 as poverty line by excluding the expenditure on vegetables, nuts, education, health etc. from the food basket of the Pay Commission Report, while as, before using the NSS based average retail prices, he marks them down to take account of the fact that the average rural consumer does not procure all of his consumption needs from the market, a part of his supply being from his own home grown stock.

E.P.W. Da Costa (1971)[58] with the help of NSS data on the consumer expenditure for the year 1963-64, estimated poverty in three rings: (1) severe destitution (2) Destitution and (3) Poverty. The three rings of poverty level are defined by the three types of "poverty line" on the basis of monthly per capita expenditure, as indicated in Table No. 23.

Table 23

Scale of Poverty Line E.P.W. Da Costa

Sr.		*Sever Distitutes*		*Destitutes*		*Poor*	
No.	*Years*	*Rural*	*Urban*	*Rural*	*Urban*	*Rural*	*Urban*
1.	1960-61	11	15	13	18	15	21
2.	1964-65	15	21	18	24	21	28
3.	1970-71	21	28	28	34	28	43
4.	1973-74	28	34	34	42	43	55

Source: Mishra, Anand Prasad, 'Rural Poverty in India', Deep and Deep Publications, New Delhi, 1988, p. 162.

On the basis of three rings of poverty, population falling under the categories of severe destination, destitution and poverty was estimated by Da Costa at 61.7 million, 104.4 million and 161.6 million corresponding to 13.2 per cent, 22.4 per cent and 34.4 per cent respectively in 1960-61.

Dandekar and Rath (1971)[59] in their widely discussed and debated study assumed that the lowest minimum physical requirement of the diet is around 2,250 calories as against FAO estimates of 1,486 calories.[60] With the help of the NSS data, they calculated that for rural areas in 1960-61, an annual per capita consumer expenditure of Rs. 170.8 was required to ensure a diet equivalent to 2,250 calories per capita per day while as in urban areas an amount of Rs. 27.7 was needed to purchase the same amount of nutrition. Thus, according to them, the urban consumer would have needed to spend roughly 59 per cent more to attain the same level of nutrition, whereas the average urban income was only 37 per cent higher. After roundingoff the consumer expenditure estimates, they calculated that Rs. 15 per capita per month in the rural areas and Rs. 22.5 in the urban areas are required to purchase the food basket consistent with calorie requirement of 2,250. Accordingly, they estimated that in 1960-61, about 33.12 per cent of the rural population and about 48.64 per cent of the urban population lived below the level of poverty. In their attempt to examine as to how the gains of development have been shared between different sections of population during the 1960's, they noted that the average consumer expenditure rose by only 4.8 per cent in the real terms in the eight year period. They also concludes that the process of development has benefitted the upper middle and the richer sections much more than the middle, lower middle and the poor sections. Under the circumstances a certain amount of inequality is inevitable'. As regards the urban population, "the lower middle and poorer sections constituting the bottom 40 per cent of the urban population have not benefitted at all by the economic development. Indeed, the evidence is that their per capita consumption has declined and greatly so among the poorest 10 per cent". Thus, they conclude that urban poverty had deepend during 1960-61 and 1968-69, although average urban income still exceeded the average rural income, albeit by a small margin. They considered a per capita annual expenditure of Rs.324 in the rural areas and Rs. 486 in the urban areas (at 1968-69 prices) as necessary for minimum level of living. On the basis of 50 per cent of urban population—in all 223.5 million people out of 532.7 million—are found to be living below the minimum level.

Madalgi[61] stated that Dandekar and Rath have not given any scientific explanation for adopting 490 g as the nutritionally required quantity of foodgrains for the urban people and 616 g for rural people. He argued that if the food grains consumption level of NSS were reliable aggregate annual consumption of food-grains derived from per capita per month figures of NSS should have been somewhere near the figure of national availability derived from production imports etc. That is not so Desai[62] stated that Dandekar and Rath are wrong in taking the average requirement. They are equally wrong in not taking into account the different requirements of different age groups, sex and so on and in basing their calculations on an all India average of Calorie intake. Further by ignoring the type, nature and intensity of activities carried on in the rural and urban areas, they have either underestimated the people falling below the poverty line in the rural areas of over-estimated the urban poor. The NSS consumer expenditure estimates for 1967-68 and 1968-69 are based on quick tabulations of unscrutinised data and have been considered uncredible even by Dandekar and Rath, for couple of reasons.[63] First, it was noted that the NSS estimates of rural per capita consumption in 1967-68 (deflated by national income deflator with 1960-61 base) was about 7 per cent below the corresponding NSS estimates in 1960-61 and about 11 per cent below the corresponding estimates in 1967-68 derived from official national accounts data. Secondly, they found that the average per capita consumption of the lowest 5 per cent rural fractile group in 1967-68 was 94 per cent of that in 1960-61, while as for top 3 per cent fractile group, the 1967-68 estimate was only 73 per cent of that in 1960-61. Such a large differential fall in the per capita consumption of the richest 3 per cent was against their a—priori—judgement. Hence, they revised the NSS estimates of per capita consumption in different sections of the rural population to firm with the official estimates of average rural consumption. It is, however, difficult to accept the authenticity of either of these two estimates without further investigation. Lastly, as stated by Shastry, the use of national income diflator to convert the current price data with 1960-61 prices is open to objection because deflating consumption by 'a deflator' which includes both consumption and investment goods is illogical. During 1960's, the prices of agricultural commodities rost at a much sharper rate than those of finished manufactures. But since, the weight of the manufactured consumables in the budget of the rural poor is likely to be much lower than the national average (which includes the rich and the poor, the urban as well as the rural sector), the national Income deflator is very much likely to have under-stated the rise in the prices paid by the rural poor. Even within the class of agricultural commodities particularly cereals, there is evidence that the average price paid by the poor rose at a faster rate than by the rich. Further, since the weight of services in the budget of the rural poor is likely to be low, the national income deflator which includes the price of services (whose index has grown at a relatively small rate), is likely to under-state the general price rise for the rural poor.

Vaidyanathan[64] by taking an income level of Rs.132 per annum to denote poverty, finds that 15.7 per cent of the rural population in 1960-61 was living in poverty. He also observes that the NSS data and the national income statistics yield different estimates of the degree of poverty as can be seen from Table No. 24. (next page)

Perusal of the Table reveals that as per NSS data, the degree of poverty has increased while as according to official series a marginal decline is recorded from 1960-61 to 1967-68.

Table 24

Poverty Estimates Rural Areas

Million People

Year	*N.S.S.*	*Official Series*
1960-61	59.5	58.0
1964-65	60.4	46 9
1967-68	67.8	57 8

Source: A. Vaidyanathan, (1974)

Bhatty adopts Sen's measure of poverty, Ps. and head count ratio to estimate the incidence of poverty among the various occupational groups in rural areas. Results of his study are summarised in Table No. 25.

Table 25

Proportions of Rural People Below the Poverty Line (1968-69)

Categories	*Rs. 15/-*	*Rs. 20/-*	*Rs. 25/-*	*Rs. 30/-*	*Rs. 35/-*
Cultivators (% age)	22.66	38.31	52.48	62.36	70.28
Agricultural Labourers (% age)	31.64	56.21	71.36	82.84	89.56
Non-agricultural Workers (% age)	21.95	39.55	55.87	69.70	79.77
All Households (% age)	24 19	42.43	56.41	67.15	75 02

Source: Bhatty, (1974), Tables 11-14, pp. 318-19.

It is observed from the Table No. 25 that for all poverty levels above Rs. 180 per capita per annum, the incidence of poverty was most severe among agricultural labourers and least among cultivators. Since the data pertain only to one year i.e., 1968-69, therefore it is not possible to show whether poverty has been increasing or not.

Sukhatme observed that nutritional requirement of 2100-2400 calor ies as adopted by most of the studies to estimate incidence of poverty in India is not the minimum but recommended average. He points out that in a population which is normally distributed with respect to height, weight, activity rate etc., half of the people will have a calorie requirement below this recommended average. By comparison of the distribution of requirements with the distribution of intake, the actual number of under-nourished persons would be smaller. According to this norm he estimates the population below the poverty line at 25 per cent and 15 per cent of the urban and rural areas. Food and Agricultural Organisation[67] estimate of poverty is based on Basal Metabolic Rate (BMR), the critical energy input required to maintain human body. The F.A.O. set a minimum limit of 1.2 BMR i.e. 1486 calories below which, is a situation of energy deprivation. The proportion of people below this critical level was estimated at about 30 per cent of total population in 1972-74.

Table 26

Incidence of Poverty in Rural India Estimates of Ahluwalia

Period	*No. of Poor (Millions)*	*% Age of Rural Population Below the Poverty Line*
1960-61	152.0	42.0
1961-62	157.0	42.3
1963-64	189.0	49.1
1964-65	198.0	50.4
1965-66	206.0	51.1
1966-67	235.0	57.4
1967-68	245.0	57.9
1968-69	227.0	53.5
1970-71	217.0	49.1
1973-74	221 0	47 6

Source: Ahluwalia, Montek S., "Rural Poverty and Agricultural Performance in India" The Journal of Development Studies, April, 1978, pp. 289-292.

Ahluwalia[68], estimates the degree of poverty in rural India for Eighteen years period from 1956-57 to 1973-74 and adopts consumer expenditure of Rs. 15 per capita per month at 1960-61 rural prices as the poverty line. He calculates equivalent poverty lines for the period under study with the help of consumer price indices for agricultural labourers. He also used the head count ratio and Sen's poverty Index Ps. to calculate the incidence of poverty. Findings of his study are presented in Table No. 26.

Analysis of Table No. 26 clearly shows that the incidence of poverty during 1960's recorded a substantial increase to as much as 241 milion people constituting 57.9 per cent of the rural population in 1967-68, However, therefore, a steady decline in the degree of poverty is seen. Ahluwalia also observed a significant inverse relationship between the performance of agricultural sector and rural poverty.

The Seventh Finance Commission[69] reflected the earliest estimates of the poverty line as being too narrow. The Commission developed a concept of an augmented poverty line according to which monthly private consumption expenditure is augmented by the per capital monthly public expenditure by each state government under various heads such as education, social welfare, roads, water supply and sanitation, health and family planning and administration of courts, jails and police. According to this augmented poverty line, the commission concludes that in 1970-71, 53 per cent of rural and 51 per cent of the urban population lived below the poverty line.

One of the avowed objectives of economic planning in India is to alleviate the poverty of its teeming millions. With the view to comprehend the nature and magnitude of poverty, planning Commission constituted a working group in 1962, which suggested that those with a per capita monthly expenditure of Rs. 20 (at 1960-61 prices) be defined as poor. But this method was not incorporated in the Fourth and Fifth Plans, which only envisaged improving the consumption level of the bottom 30 per cent people. Only in the Sixth Plan[70] was the parameter of poverty clearly defined and methodology spelt out in the technical note of the plan documented. Sixth Plan adopted the physical survival definition of poverty and identified poverty line as the mid-point of a monthly per capital expenditure of a class having a daily calorie intake of 2,435 per person in rural areas and 2,095 calorie per person in urban areas which worked out to Rs. 76 in rural areas and Rs. 88 in urban areas at 1979-80 prices. Those spending less than these sums were declared as poor. On this criteria the Planning Commission found that in 1979-80, 3,168 million persons constituting 48.4 per cent of the country's total population are living below the poverty line. Out of the total population of the poor, 260 million are residing in the rural areas and 57 million in the urban areas. In relative terms, 50.7 per cent of the rural population and 40.3 per cent of the urban population are categorised as poor. In 1984-85[71] poor population is estimated at 272.7 million of 36.9 per cent of the total population, out of which 222.2 million or 39.9 per cent are living in the rural areas and 50.5 million constituting 27.7 per cent are residing in the urban areas. In the seventh Five Year Plan, poverty line is estimated around Rs. 6,400 per annum of household income or approximately Rs. 107 per capita per month at 1984-85 prices. On this criteria, the Seventh Plan envisages the percentage of population with consumption standard below the poverty line to come down to 25.8 per cent by 1989-90. In absolute terms, the number of poor persons is expected to fall from 273 million in 1984-85 to 211 million in 1989-90. For the rural and urban areas, the respective figures are 168.6 million (28.2 per cent) and 42.2 million (19.3 per cent). Plan projections also suggest that the percentage of people below poverty line is expected to decline to 10 per cent by 1994-95 and further to a level of 5 per cent in the year 2000.

Authenticity of these estimates of Planning Commission regarding the incidence of Poverty has come under scathing criticism. Controversy centres around the number of persons estimated at 57 million by the Planning Commission to have crossed the poverty line because of the rise in their real incomes during 1980-81 and 1981-82. According to Raj Krishna after taking into account the impact of IRDP and NREP as well as the growth of GNP "the maximum number of poverty line crossers in the first two years of the Sixth Plan could only be 7.7 million and not 57 million". Therefore, his estimate of population in poverty is around 331 million i.e., 48.8 per cent of total population.[72] Vasant Gumaste observed that since under IRDP and NREP transfer of technology, assets and service (TAS) has tended to benefit the top layers of income category therefore, the likely number of families who have crossed over the poverty line should be about 1.4 million or 7 million persons.[73] Sundaram and Tendulkar conclude that 11 million persons plausibly have been pushed up above the poverty line by 1981-82. However, keeping in view, the results of 1981 census and the extent of under-estimation, "the incidence of poverty in 1981-82 would be 46.50 per cent of 329 million poor instead of 41.5 per cent or 282 million poor as estimated by the Planning Commission".[74] It may be pointed out that the incidence of poverty over the years has been moving up and down following the trend of food-grain production. This fact has also been admitted by the Planning Commission. The poverty level has been high in years when the agricultural production particularly food-grains have been high. Since food-grain constitute a major part of the consumption expenditure, the levels of the living poor move up in good agricultural years and move down during bad harvest. It is thus seen that in 1972-73 when food-grain output was lower at 97 million tonnes as against 105 million tonnes in 1971-72, the poverty line jumped up to 51.5 per cent. In 1977-78, when the food-grain production had gone up to 126.4 million tonnes from 121 million tonnes in 1976-77, the poverty level came down to 48.3 per cent. Again in 1983-84, when total production increased to 152.4 million tonnes as against 129.5 million tonnes in 1982-83, the poverty line came down to 42.6 per cent. If this trend is followed, it would mean that in 1984-85, when the food-grain production decreased to 146 million tonnes, the poverty line would have jumped up and not falling down to 36.9 as estimated by the Planning Commission. Further, in view of the overall performances of the Indian economy during the last four decades, it is reasonable to conclude that the expectation of the planning

Table 27

A Comparative Statement Showing Different Estimates of Rural Poverty in India

Sr. No.	*Year*	*Organisation/ Researcher*	*Estimated Number of Poor (Millions)*	*% of Rural Population Below Poverty Line*	*Definition of Poverty Based on*
1	*2*	*3*	*4*	*5*	*6*
1.	1960-61	Dandekar and Rath	135.0	40.0	Rs. 1.80 per cent at 1960-61 prices yielding a minimum of 2,250 calories per day.
2.		Ahluwalia	152.0	42.0	Rs. 189 p.c., c.e., p.a., at 1960-61 prices.
		Vaidyanathan	213.3	59.5	Rs. 240 p.c., c e., p.a., at 1960-61 prices.
		Ojha	184.2	51.8	Rs. 216 p.c., c.e., p a., at 1960-61 prices.
3.	1961-62	Ahluwalia	157.0	42.3	Rs. 180 p.c., c.e., p.a., at 1960-61 prices.

4.	1962-63	NIRD	166.0	44 9	The regression equation between NDP from agriculture and Ahluwalia's time series estimates of incidence of poverty.
5.	1963-64	E.P.W. De Costa	161.0	34.6	There types of classification, destitutes, severe destitutes and poor based on a minimum per capita expenditure per annum.
		D.S. Minhas	221.0	57.8	Two alternative levels of Rs. 240 and 200 per capita annual consumption expenditure at 1960-61 prices.
		Ahluwalia	189.0	49.1	Above mentioned criterion.
6.	1964-65	Vaidyanathan	235.7	60.0	As mentioned above Rs. 240 p.c., p.a., c.e.
		Bardhan	17·.4	51.6	Rs. 180 p.c., c.e., p,a., at 1960-61,
		Ahluwalia	198.0	50 4	Above mentioned criterion.
7.	1965-66	Ahluwalia	205.0	51.1	Above mentioned criterion.
8.	1966-67	Ahluwalia	235.0	57.4	Above mentioned criterion.

(Contd.)

1	2	3	4	5	6
9.	1967-68	Ahluwalia	241.0	57.9	Above mentioned criterion.
		Dandekar & Rath	166.4	40.0	Above mentioned criterion.
		Vaidyanathan	—	67.8	Above mentioned criterion
		Minhas	210.0	50.6	Rs. 240 p.c , c.e., p a.
		Ojha	289.0	70.0	Estimates of minimum desirable income i e., Rs. 216 to Rs. 480 per annum.
10.	1968-69	Ahluwalia	227.0	53.5	Above mentioned criterion.
11.	1969-70	A FICCI	218.3	41 2	Rs. 240, p c., c.e., p.a , at 1960-61 prices.
		NIRD	196 0	42.2	Earlier mentioned criterion.
12.	1970-71	Ahluwalia	217.0	49.1	Earlier mentioned criterion.
		IIPC	198.9	45.0	Rs. 336 p.c , c.e., p a.
13.	1971-72	NIRD	183.0	41.5	Earlier mentioned criterion.
14.	1972-73	NIRD	212.0	47.2	Earlier mentioned criterion.
		Planning Commission	200.0	35.8	Rs. 480 p.c., c.e., p a , at 1972-73 prices.

15.	1973-74	Ahluwalia	221 0	47 6	Earlier mentioned criterion.
		IIPO	208 0	44·8	Rs. 516 p.c., c e., p.a.
16.	1974-75	NIRD	232.0	50.1	Earlier mentioned criterion.
17.	1975-76	NIRD	225.0	47.7	Earlier mentioned criterion.
18.	1976-77	NIRD	236.0	45.2	Earlier mentioned criterion
19.	1977-78	Planning Commission	251.7	50.8	Rs. 741 60 p.c., c.e., p a , (2400 calories, per day).
		IIPO	246.4	50.8	Rs. 780 p c., c.e., p.a., 24 calories per day.
20.	1979-80	Planning Commission	259.6	50.7	Rs. 7 6 per person per month at current prices (2400 calories per day).

p.c.=per capital, c e =consumer expenditure, p.a.=per annum.

Commission to bring down percentage of population below the poverty line to 5 per cent is more a wishful thining.

Precisely, the findings of the various studies regarding the incidence of poverty in rural India are summarized in Table No. 27.

References

1. Buch, M.A., 'Economic Life Ancient India', Baroda, 1924, pp. 192-193.
2. Bandhopadyaya, N.C., "Economic Life and Progress in Ancient India", Calcutta, 1925, pp. 276-277.
3 Dass, S.K., "Economic History of Ancient India", Calcutta, 1929.
4 Ghosal, U.N., "Contributions to the Study of the Hindu Revenue System", Calcutta, 1929, pp. 273-9. Cited in Jha, D.N., "Studies in Early Indian Economic History", Anupam Publications, Delhi, 1980, p. 8.
5. Ghosal, U.N , Cited in Jha, D.N., "Studies in Early Indian Economic History", p. 8.
6. Altekar, A S., "The Rashtrakutas and their Times", Poona, 1934, p. 396.
7. Morris, D. Morris and Steen, Burton, "The Economic History of India. A Bibliographic Essay", Journal of Economic History XXI, (1961), p. 182, Cited in Jha, D.N., p. 11.
8. Basu, B.D., "The Rise of Christian Power in India", Calcutta, 1931, Cited in Jha, D.N., p. 11.
9. Bose, A.N., "Social and Rural Economy of Northern India", 600, BC—A.D. 200, Calcutta, 1942-45, Cited in Jha, D.N., p. 18.
10. Sharma, R.S., "A Survey of Land System in India from 200 B.C. to A.D. 650", JBRS, XLIV, (1958), Cited in Jha, D.N., p. 26.
11. Cited in Jha, D.N., p. 26.
12 Cited in Jha, D.N., p. 2.
13. Niyogi, Pushpa, "Contribution to the Economic History of Northern India from Tenth to Twelfth Century A.D.", Calcutta, 1962, Cited in Jha, D.N., p. 27.
14. Gopal, L., "Economic Life in Northern India", Delhi, Cited in Jha, D.N., p. 27.

15. Cited in Economic History of India, 1757-1947 by Rajan, V. Sundra, East and West Book House, Baroda, 1955, p. 12.
16. *Cit. op.*, p. 20.
17. Majumdar, R.C., and Others, *cit. op.*, p. 20
18. Report of the Indian Industrial Commission (1918), Cit in Economic History of India by Sundra Rajan, p. 4.
19. Cited by Kuezynski, Jurgan, "Conditions of Workers", (1880-1950). In "Economic History of India, 1857-1956", Alied Publishers, Private Limited, New Delhi, 1965, p. 619, by Singh, V B.
20. *Cit. op*, p. 620.
21. Banerjee, P., "A Study of Indian Economics", 5th ed, 1940, pp. 199-200.
22. Ganguli, B N., "Indian Economic Thought", Nineteenth Century Perspective", Tata McGraw Hill Publishing Co. Ltd., New Delhi, 1977, p. 38.
23. *Ibid.*, p. 148.
24. *Ibid.*, p. 148.
25. *Ibid.*, p. 184.
26. *Ibid.*, p. 186.
27. *Ibid.*, p. 190.
28. Fuchs, V.R. (1967), "Redefining Poverty and Redistributing Income", the Public Interest, Summer, pp. 88-95.
29. Dhaudari, Pramit, "The Indian Economy—Poverty and Development", Vikas Publishing House Pvt. Ltd, New Delhi, 1978, p. 196.
30. *op. cit.*, pp. 180-181.
31. Dandekar, V.M., and Rath, N., 'Poverity in India', Economic and Political Weekly, Bombay, 1971, p. 27.
32. Srinivasan, T.N., and Bardhan, P.K. (ed.), "Poverty and Income Distribution in India", Statistical Publishing Society, Calcutta, 1974.
33. Srinivasan, *et. al.*
34 Dandekar and Rath, N., (1974), p. 27.
35. Bardhan, P., "On the Minimum Level of Living of the Rural Poor", Indian Economic Review, 1970, April.
36. Lydall, F.H., "The Inequality of Indian Incomes", Economic Weekly Special Number, June, 1960.
37. Iyengar, N.S, and Mukherjee, M., 'A note on the Derivation of Size Distribution of Personal Household Income from a size—Distribution of Consumer Expenditure, (Mimco, 1961).
38. Reserve Bank of India, "Distribution of Income in the Indian Economy, 1953-54 to 1956-57", Reserve Bank of India, Bulletin, September (1962).
39. National Council of Applied Economic Research.
    (i) Urban Income and Saving, New Delhi, 1962.
    (ii) All-India Consumer Expenditure Survey, Vol. I & II, New Delhi, 1966.

40. Ojha, P.D., and Bhatta, V V , "Pattern of Income Distribution in India, 1953-54 to 1963-65", in Srinivasan and Bardhan (eds.), Poverty and Income Distribution in India, pp. 163-66.
41. Ranadiv, K.R . "Distribution of Income-trends Since Planning", Paper Presented to Seminar on Income Distribution held at the Indian Statistical Institute, Calcutta, February, 1973.
42. Madalgi, S.S., "Population and Food Supply in India", p. 81.
43 Tendulkar, Suresh, D., "Economic Incqualities and Poverty in India: Interpretative Overview", Cited in Brahmananda and Panchmukhi (eds.), 'The Development Process of the Indian Ecc-nomy', Himalaya Publishing House, Delhi, 1987, p 122.
44. NCAER, "All India Household Survey of Income Savings and Consumer Expenditure", December, 1972.
45. Dandekar, V.M., and Rath, N., "Poverty in India—Dimension and Trende", Economic and Political Weekly, January 2, 1981, p. 40
46. Planning Commission, Goverment of India, "The Sixth Five Year Plan", (1980-85).
47. *Op. cit.*, p. 123.
48. *Op. cit.*, p. 124.
49. Iyengar, N.S., and Brahamananda, P.R., "Estimated Distribution Parameters and their Behaviour in the Post Independence Period", "The Development Process of the Indian Economy", Himalaya Publishing House, Delhi, 1987, pp. 82-105.
50. Iyengar, N S. and Bhattacharya, N., "On the Effects of Differentials in the Consumer Price Index, on Measures of Inequality", Sankhya Series B, Vol. 27, 1965, pp. 47-56.
51. Vaidyanathan, A., "Some aspects of Inequalities in Living Standards in Rural India", in Srinivasan, T.N. and Bardhan, P.K. (eds.), in 1974, *op. cit.*, pp. 214-241.
52. Iyengar, N.S., and Jain, L.R., "A Method of Estimating Income Distribution", Economic and Political Weekly, Vol. IX, No. 41, 1974, pp. 2103-2109.
53. Radhakrishna, R , and Sharma, Atul, "Inflation and Disparities in Levels of Living", Indian Economic Journal, Vol. 23, No. 4, 1976, pp. 364-373.
54. Iyengar, N S.. and Suryanarayana, M.H., "On Growth and Equity in Indian Planning during 1961-62 to 1973-74", The Indian Eco-nomic Journal, Vol. 33, No. 4, April-June, 1986, pp. 55-83.
55. Ojha, P.D., "A Configuration of Indian Poverty, Inequality and Levels of Living", Reserve Bank of India, Bulletin, January, 1970.
56. Minhas, B.S., "Rural Poverty, Land Redistribution and Develop-ment", Indian Economic Review, Vol. V, No. 1, April, 1970.
57. Bardhan, P.K., "The Green Revolution and Agricultural Labourers", Economic and Political Weekly, Special Number, 1970.

58. Da Costa, E.P.W., "A Portrait of Indian Poverty", in Challenge of Poverty in India, A J. Fonseca (ed.), Delhi, 1971, p. 51.
59. Dandekar, V.M., and Rath Nilkanth, "Poverty in India", Indian School of Political Economy, Bombay, 1971.
60 Food and Agricultural Organisation, "Energy and Protein Requirements : Report of a joint FAO/WHO ad hoc expert Committee, Geneva, 1973, p. 36.
61. Madalgi, S.S. "Poverty in India—a Comment", Economic and Political Weekly, February 20, 1971, p. 505.
62. Desai, S S.M., "Poverty in India—The Magnitude of the Problem", The Economic Times, Friday, Nov. 28, 1980.
63. Shastry, S.A.R., "A Survey of Literature on Poverty, Income Distribution and Development", Artha Vijnana, Vol. XXII, No. 1, March 1980, Section III.
64. Vaidyanathan, A., "Some Aspects of Inequalities in Living Standards in Rural India", in Poverty and Income Distribution in India (ed.), Srinivasan and Baidhan, Statistical Publishing Society, Calcutta, 1974, pp. 215-241.
65. Bhatty, I.Z, "Inequality and Poverty in Rural India in Poverty and Income Distribution in India", (ed.), by Srinivasan and Baidhan, Statistical Publishing Society, Calcutta, 1974, pp. 291-336.
66. Sukhatme, P.V., "Malnutrition and Poverty", 9th, L.B S. Memorial Lecture, ICAR, New Delhi.
67. U.N., F.A O., and W.H.O., "Energy and Protein Requirements", Geneva, 1973, p. 36.
68. Ahluwalia, Montek S, "Rural Poverty and Agricultural Performance in India", The Journal of Development Studies, April 1978, pp. 289-92.
69. The Economic Times, Wednesday, March 5, 1986.
70. Governmet of India, Planning Commission, Sixth Five Year Plan, 1980-85, New Delhi, 1981, pp. 51-53.
71. Government of India, Planning Commission, Seventh Five Year Plan, 1985-90, New Delhi, Oct. 1985, Vol. I, pp. 32-33.
72. Raj, Krishna, Growth, Investment and Poverty in Midterm Appraisal of Sixth Plan, Economic and Political Weekly, Nov. 19, 1983, p. 1976.
73 Vasant Gumaste, Is Poverty Disappearing Financial Express, June 21, 1983.
74. Sunderam, K., and Tendulkar, S.D, "Poverty in the Mid Term Appraisal, Economic and Political Weekly, Nov. 5-13, 1983, p. 1935.

4

Summary and Conclusions

Phenomenon of poverty is not only collosal in its extent but also multi-faceted. The stark poverty is apparent and does not need the criteria and deeper analysis to recognise it. But the movement away from raw poverty and misery does pose the problems of identification of the poor and diagnosis and measurement of poverty. These problems of conceptualisation and measurement of poverty have opened up a never ending debate for, poverty is too complex a phenomenon cutting across a myriad of economic, social, cultural, political and psychological factors. Therefore, controversies persists as how to define and measure poverty.

Amongst different approaches opinions centering around the 'Cultural triats of poor', 'biological inadequacies' and 'relative deprivation' constitute the core of widely discussed concepts of poverty. Oscar Lewis, one of the prominent protagonists of identifying the poor on the basis of their characteristics, behaviour patterns and other attributes, defines 'culture of poverty' as a permanent way of life that develops among the poor people. Similarly, Rossi and Blum have identified the critical feature of the poor. According to their view, culture of poverty is not only sustained by external environment but also by internal systems of values and preferences and inter-personal relationships that have a validity and life of their aim and that are capable of persisting well after the external circumstances have been modified or changed together. 'Poverty' according to them "creates pathologies that block the ability to adopt at non-pathological situation". Since the 'culture of poverty' concept highlights the negative traits of only the poor people and ignores the 'poverty of culture' of the affluent who deliberately keep their fellow citizens poor therefore, this view is less a culture of poverty, than the sociology of the underclass. The culture of poverty, concept defies measurement of a 'change' therefore social scientists attempted to define poverty in terms and of a single quantifiable characteristic that all poor families only poor families possess.

This necessitated the search for an objective definition of poverty with the attributes of measurability, objectivity comparability and sensitivity to changes. Accordingly in defining poverty emphasis shifted from cultural attributes of the poor to his biological needs in terms of minimum food requirements, biological conceptualization of poverty has two varients viz., (a) subsistance criterion ; and (b) nutritional criterion.

According to subsistence criterion, poverty is a situation which denies minimum food and shelter necessary to maintain/sustain life. The difficulty with this criterion is that the dividing line between the 'poor' and 'non-poor' is neither permanent nor uniform but changes both in space and time because it is conditioned by multiplicity of factors such as physical and climatic environment as well as the social structure and culture of the consuming unit. Besides, minimum requirements are also influenced by age, sex, vocation and other attributes of the consuming unit which make standardisation of a 'basket of necessities' a difficult proposition.

Nutritional criterion associates poverty with the nutritional inadequacy and implies a minimum calorie intake below which there is under-nutrition along with some 'norm' for determining the minimum cost of an adequate diet. This criterion is also defective in as much as the quality and variety of food to be recommended to meet nutritional goals is dictated by the social conscience and customs of the consuming unit. There is also a dispute about using the average requirement based on the reference individual and equivalences for age and sex as the criterion to be used for judging the nutritional status of an entire population. Further, the criterion of nutritional adequacy in terms of minimum intake of calories per head per day as recommended by various organisations and/or researchers lack agreement and the suggested minimum calories These anomalies obviously are reflected in the estimates of incidence of poverty, and also in the policy measures to alleviate poverty.

The inequality approach to defining the poverty stresses that inadequality and poverty are congruant and hence co-terminus with each other. This approach emphasises that inequality is concerned with the relative position of income groups to each other, hence poverty cannot be understood by isolating the poor and treating them as special group. It visualizes the society as a consisted of a series of stratified income layers and stresses that poverty is connected with how the bottom layers fare relative to the rest of the society. It is while true that inequality and poverty are not unrelated to each other but they do not subsume each other. Reduction in income inequality may not, correspond to decline in poverty. Similarly, poverty may be intensified with the reduction in the level of income even when pattern of income distribution has remained unchanged. Further, this approach ignores hunger and starvation, the two most important parameters of poverty.

Concept of poverty in terms of relative deprivation refers to conditions wherein people lack the basic elements to life and well-being (Elaboration of this concept suggests that it is not possession of relatively less resources but only the incapacity to have the types of dietes, participate in activities and enjoy living conditions and amenities which are customary in the society which would indicate that people are in poverty. Besides the deprivation of resources, the concept also embraces the 'feeling' of deprivation connected with the want of opportunities to catch up with the better privileged sections of society. The concept is useful to understand poverty as a socio-economic and non-political phenomenon. However, it forms the weak basis of conceptualisation of poverty for absolute deprivation constitutes the central idea of poverty.

Operative for policy definition of poverty reflects a balancing of community's capabilities and desires. Determination of an appropriate relationship between policy and policy is a difficult task for, it is influenced by multiplicity of factors including economic and non-economic and therefore, may reflect objectives other than only the eradication of poverty. It must also be remembered that inescapable poverty is still poverty.

Analysis of various approaches to defining poverty clearly reveals that the notion of poverty contains both absolute and relative dimensions, static and dynamic aspects and stocks and flow elements. The Biological and inequality approaches contain all these dimensions, aspects and elements, despite many infirmities, with suitable refinements constitute the basis of most of the studies aiming the measurement and eradication of poverty.

Poverty is measured either with the help of some 'objective criteria' or a 'normative' norm, the former essentially measures inequality and later absolute poverty.

Income is considered to be the best measure of an economic position of the economic unit particularly of economic position is taken to mean the potential buying power rather than the actual purchase of consumption goods. Although the actual level of consumption determines the standard of living, yet the extent of buying power and the actual level of consumption are highly correlated. Theoritical studies of income distribution and techniques were originally initiated by

Pareto (1897), however, contribution of Gini and Lorenz (1905) is of great importance. The works of Gilbert (1942) and Brown and Atkinson (1970) in this field are praise worthy. Atkinson's measure is explicitly related to an underlying social welfare formation and is quite useful for comparing or ranking alternative distributions. There are also measures borrowed from information theory such as the index development by Theil (1967).

The most widely used measure of inequality of income distribution is the concentration ratio developed by Gini. It is the ratio of area between the Lorenz Curve and the 'egalitarian line' to the area of the triangle below the egalitarian. The, Lorenze Curve relates to the cumulative proportion of consuming units (families) to the cumulative proportion of income received, assuming that the consuming units are arranged in an ascending order of income. The 'egalitarian line' shows the situation where each consuming unit (family) receive the same income. If each family receives the same income. If each family receives the same income, the Lorenz Curve coincides with the 'egalitarion line' and the concentration ratio assumes value zero. On the other hand if a single family receives all incomes, the concentration ratio becomes unity. The concentration ratio is criticised on the basis of its assumption that "equal importance may be attached to equal absolute difference of income", even though one of the difference is taken between too low incomes and others between too high incomes. Further, this measure is considered misleading because a highly concentrated income distribution (in the sense of high, single peak in a frequency distribution of families to size of income) will mean a more equal distribution (in sense of dispersion) than a low plateau distribution, with arithmatic mean equal for the two distribution. Despite these critical observations concentration ratio is perhaps the best single overall measure of inequality.

The other popular measures are the quintiles i.e., the share in total income of 20 per cent of families starting at the bottom. The shares of the quantiles of families in total income do not yield a single overall measure. If the shares of the lowest (bottom) and highest (top) quitiles are considered, the ommission of the influences of items that fall outside the related range is a serious disadvantage for the study of inequality of income distribution.

Two other popular measures are the coefficient of variation and the Standard Deviation of the logs of income. The co-efficient of variation is an appropriate measure if only the absolute differences of incomes are to be estimated. But it is very sensitive to changes in the shape of frequency distribution of income. Moreover, for the purpose of inequality comparisons, it is of dubious value depending as it does on means. Two distributions with the same standard deviations will yield different co-efficient of variations due to differences in means. The standard deviations of the logarithms of incomes may be appropriate is only the percentage differences are to be calculated. It becomes a desirable measure of inequality if income is lognormally dissributed. This measure is also very sensitive to the changes in the frequency distribution of income.

Another objcctive measure of poverty is the head Count ratio. This measure is completely insensitive to the extent of the aggregate shortfall in income (from the poverty line) as well as to the distribution of incomes amongst the poor. Inspite of its short comings, this measure is widely used due to its simplicity and the idea which it gives about the magnitude of the problem.

In view of the deficiencies in these objective (positive) measures of poverty, Prof. A.K. Sen suggested anothet measure of inequality which takes into account not only the number of people below the poverty line but also the amounts by which the incomes of the poor fall short of the specified poverty level. It also suggests that bigger the short fall from the poverty level, the greater should be the weight per unit of that short fall in the poverty measure. Precisely, this measure lays greater emphasis on the distribution of income among the poor, that is, it attempts to measure the depth of poverty.

According to the normative measures. 'Poverty line' delineates the poor from the non-poor. A person is in poverty when his standard of living falls below minimum acceptable level of living. This is turn of raises questions about the minimum acceptable level of living. The standard of living is a multidimensional concept. The various commodities an individual consume's and activities he engages in or could engage in, all form part of his standard of living. Given this multidimensionality, the first step in specifying of poverty specification of a minimum acceptable level along each of a the different dimensions. This is in itself problematic, there may be no clear agreement on a sharp divide between poor and non-poor. There may be a greater degree of agreement along the nutritional dimension (although even here there is a range of possibilities), disagreements are more likely along non-nutritional dimensions such as clothing and housing or, even more so, other items of expenditure such as entertainment. Accordingly, it is not inconsistent or incoherent to say that two individuals, one in a poor country and one in a rich country, are both in poverty and equally so, even though the income level of the person in rich country is many times that of the person in the poor country.

These conceptual issues aside, poverty line at the operational level is estimated with the help of two methods. One is to specify minimum requirements for both food and non-food items and to then calculate the amount of income necessary to purchase these at current prices. The other approach involves the identification of the nutritionally 'minimum balanced diet' for an average person in terms of the value of calorie intake which then is costed and blown up by a ratio of food to total expenditure (Engels Coefficient) inorder to account for necessary minimum expenditure on non-food items. This approach provide not only an index of poverty but also equips to have better insight into the structure of poverty and thereby, meets the policy requirements of any poverty alleviation programme.

This approach is now the basis for poverty-line calculations in many developing countries including India. There is, however, lack of consensus on the minimum per-capita requirement of calories because number of variables like age, sex, body weight, level of activity etc., effect the energy expenditure. Another, limitation of this method appears due to the divergence between expert judgement and actual consumption behaviour which is conditioned by ignorance, social conventions etc. Further, the degree of arbitrariness in case of non-food items may be more pronounced due to the climatic and social factors. Thus, a uniform norm either in terms of food basket which would provide minimum subsistance or its equivalent in money terms (because of price variation) would not be appropriate for the country as a whole.

Analysis of incidence of poverty in India conclusively reveal the prevalence of poverty in varying degrees in the Pre-British period. During the British period, it was not only deep but was deepening. In the post-independence era, poverty alleviation automatically turned out to be one of the major objectives of the policies, aiming at the socio-economic transformation of the country. Soon it was realised that growth by itself was not likely to reduce inequality and reduce poverty. This realisation necessitated the comprehension and deeper analysis of poverty in its varied manifestations. Thus, investigations into the phenomenon of poverty centered around two inter-related themes, viz., inequality and poverty.

One of the earliest attempts to know the nature of income inequality is associated with the report of the Committee on "Distribution of Income and Levels of Living". Set up by the government of India in 1960 under the Chairmanship of Prof. P.C. Mahalnobis. The Committee submitted its report in 1964, but thereafter no similar effort was made to probe into this issue in-depth. Reserve Bank of India, National Council of Applied Economic Research and some individual researchers notably Ojha and Bhatt (1963-64 and 1964-65), K.R. Ranadive (1961-62), Madalgi (1971) have examined the pattern of income distribution at different points of time with the help of data, from different sources. All these studies suggest that during the period under review, income inequalities in the country were quite pronounced, however, distribution of income in rural areas was less skewed than in the urban areas. Tendulkar observed that the Gini Co-efficient for the rural population decreased and for urban population increased during 1953-54 to 1975-76, a movement in the opposite deduction occurred.

With the view to have a better perception of changes in the levels of living, the data made available from the National Sample Survey Organisation have been examined rigorously by Dandekar and Rath (1960-61 to 1967-68) Tendulkar (1953-54 to 1975-76). Iyengar and Brahmananda (1950-51 to 1983-84), Iyengar and Bhattacharya, Vaidyanathan, and the Planning Commission. The broad conclusions of these studies are :

(a) Inequality is more proncounced in the pattern of income distribution than in the distribution of consumer expenditure;

(b) Degree of inequality in income as well as expenditure is higher in urban than in the rural areas of the country; and

(c) Inequality in the distribution of income and expenditure in both the rural and urban sectors has declined at current prices while as at constant prices no firm trend is evident.

It must be kept in mind that the data base of these studies are fragile and infirm and therefore, their conclusions are incomparable. Further, derivation of size distibution of income by most of the studies from the consumption expenditure data collected by the National Sample Survey is based on the assumption that the degree of inequality in income distribution would be the same as in case of the pattern of consumption expenditure is smaller than for incomes because of various reasons. Isseus pertaining to the choice of a correct price deflator for purposes of inter-temporal and spatial comparisons of income and consumption expenditure data have remained unresolved and therefore, researches reflection of a price deflator has been conditioned by the subjectivity/bias and this has made their conclusions incomparable studies on income distribution pattern have combined MSS data with income tax data which are inadequate and unsatisfactory and this has reduced the authencity of their observations.

Along with the analysis of the pattern of income and expenditure distribution various estimates have also been made of the poverty line and of the proportion of population subsisting below it. One of the earliest studies is by a study group of the Planning Commission of India, it estimated Rs. 20 per month of 1960-61 prices as the bare minimum level of living, with no allowance for any expenditure on health and education. Several other estimates broadly confirm this. In his various studies Bardhan (1974) uses Rs. 15 for rural and Rs. 18 for urban areas to delineate poverty line while Dandekar and Rath (1971) suggest the same figure for rural but a higher figure of Rs. 22.5 for urban areas (all at 1960-61 prices). On the basis of these estimates Bardhan has suggested that in 1968-69 as many as 54 per cent of the rural population were below the poverty line along with 41 per cent of the urban population. Dandekar and Rath have reversed rural/urban populations, finding the relatively greater incidence of poverty to be in urban areas with 48.64 per cent of the population below the level of poverty as against 33.12 per cent in rural areas. Ojha draws the line of demarcation between poor and non-poor at Rs. 18 per month. In the rural areas and Rs. 11 in the urban areas and estimates that in 1960-61, approximately 51.8 per cent of rural population as 184.2 million people and 7.6 per cent or 6 million people in urban areas lived in poverty. Minhas adopts the figure of Rs. 2.40 per person per annum as a poverty line for the urban areas and Rs. 200 for rural population and arrives at the conclusion that people below the poverty line of Rs. 200 decreased from 173 million in 1956-57 to 154 million in 1967-68, that is, from 52.4 per cent to 37.1 per cent of rural population.

Vaidyanathan takes an income level of Rs. 132 per annum to denote poverty and finds that 15.7 per cent of rural population in 1960-61 were living inpoverty. Bhatty uses Sen's measure of poverty and head count ratio to estimate the incidence of poverty and observes that for all poverty levels above Rs. 180 per capita per annum, the incidence of poverty was most severe among agricultural labourers, and least among cultivators. Ahluwalia estimates the degree of poverty in rural India by using head count ratio and Sen's poverty index and concludes that the poverty line of Rs.15 per capita per month incidence of poverty increased to 57.9 per cent of rural population in 1967-68 and thereafter declined to 47.6 per cent in 1973-74.

Planning Commission, Government of India defined for the first time the parameter of poverty and spelt out the methodology in the technical note of the Sixth Five Year Plan. It adopted the physical survival definition and identified poverty line as the mid-point of a monthly per capita expenditure of a class having daily calorie intake of 2,435 per person in rural areas and 2,095 calorie per person in urban areas which worked to Rs. 76 for rural areas and Rs. 88 for urbon areas at 1979-80 prices and found that in 1979-80, 48.4 per cent of the country's population, 50.7 per cent of the rural population and 40.3 per cent of the urban population were living below the poverty line. In 1984-85, 37 per cent of total population, 40 per cent and 27.7 per cent of rural and urban population respectively were living below the poverty level. The Seventh Five Year Plan demarcates the poverty line around Rs. 6,400 per annum per household or about Rs. 107 per capita per month at 1984-85 prices and estimate that population below the poverty line will come down to 25.8 per cent by 1989-90 while as it would be around 28 2 per cent and 19.3 per cent in rural and urban areas respectively. Planning Commission optimistic projections envisage the proportion of population to fall below the poverty line to 10 per cent by 1994-95 and 5 per cent in the year 2000 A.D. Estimates of Planning Commission have come under the scathing criticism of Raj Krishna, Vasant Gumaste, Sundaram and Tendulkar who have found defects in the Planning Commission calculations of poverty line crosses at 57 million people during the first two years of Sixth Five Year Plan 1980-81, 1981-82) and have worked out this figure at about 71 million people. Accordingly their estimates reveal that the percentage of population below the poverty line in 1983-84 ranges between 46.5 to 48.8 and not 41.5 as suggested by Planning Commission.

These studies on the delineation of the poverty line and the Calculation of population below it have different reference dates which account for variations in the estimates. Further, the minimum necessary calorie intake is variously defined, usually between 2100 and 2400 per day. The composition of the diet incorporating the minimum nutritional requirements. Similarly varies and in a country of the geographic size and ethnic complexity of India any single diet can only be an approximation. The prices used in costing the diet and the expenditure distribution into which the poverty-line is projected are similarly liable to variation. For these reasons no single figure can be adopted with certainity and precision. Another criticism of the methodology is based on Sukhatme's argument that the recommended nutritional requirement (of say 2500 or 2200 calories) is recommended average and not a minimum which in itself suggests that in a population which is normally distributed with respect to height, weight, activity rate etc., half the people will have a calorie requirement below this recommended average. It is only by comprising the distribution of requirements against the distribution of intake that are can find the actual number of undernourished persons. A further source of inaccuracy in the conventional methodology for estimating the poverty line relates to the practice of blowing up the estimated cost of the necessary diet by a fixed ratio between food and non-food expenditure as obtained from consumption surveys. This pre-supposes that the recorded levels of food and non-food expenditure fall short of their basic minimum standards in the same proportion. The direction of the bias of this, however, cannot be easily established but its existence cannot be denied. Yet another source of error in the estimate of the proportion of the population in poverty, lies in the failure to capture intra-family inequities. Even families above the poverty line may include members who are seriously under-nourished. Women, children and old people most often come into this category.

Thus, the poverty line like any other composite index, inspite of its usefulness in indicating the general magnitude of poverty cannot claim to be an accurate and precise measuring rod. It is therefore, important that its methodology be standarised and operational significance enhence through continuous research.

Bibliography

Agrawala, A.N., *Indian Economy*, Vikas Publishing House, New Delhi, 1979.

Atkinson, A.B., (Ed.). *Wealth, Income and Inequality* Penguin, London, 1973.

Atkinson, A.B., *The Economics of Inequality*. Oxford University Press, 1975.

Brahmanada, P.R., and Panchmukhi, V.R.C., *The Development Process of the Indian Economy*" Himalaya Publishing House, Delhi, 1987.

Buch, M.A., "Economic Life in Ancient India, Baroda, 1924.

Bajaj, J.L., and Shastri, C., Rural Poverty Issues and options: Print House (India), Lucknow (1984).

Chaudhuri, Pramit. The Indian Economy Poverty and Develop ment, Vikas Publishing House, New Delhi (1978).

Dandekar, V.M., and Rath, N., Poverty in India, Indian School of Political Economy, Bombay, 1971.

Dantwala, M.L , Poverty in India Then and Now, 1870-1970. The Macmillan Company of India, Ltd , Delhi, 1973.

Dutt, Palma, R., India To-day. Manishia Granthalaya (P) Ltd., Calcutta, 1979.

Elhance, D.N., "Fundamentals of Statistics". Kitab Mahal, Allahabad, (1977).

Lack, J. Murray, The War on Malnutrition and Poverty, New York, Herper and Brothers (1946).

Gadgil, D.R., "Sholapur City—Socio-Economic Studies", Asia Publishing House (1968).

Mellor, J.W., and Desai, G.M. (Ed.), Agricultural Change and Rural Poverty, Variation on a Theme by Dharam Narain, Oxford University Press, Bombay.

Minhas, B.S., "Planning and the Poor", S. Chand and Company, New Delhi, 1976.

Mishra, A.P., Rural Poverty in India, Deep and Deep Publications, New Delhi.

Moynihan, Daniel, P., On Understanding Poverty, Basic Books Inc. Publishers.

Myrdal, Gunnar., Asian Drama, An Inquiry into the Poverty of Nations, 20th Century Fund, Pantheon Books, New York, 1968.

Peatman, J.G., Introduction to Applied Statistics. Harper and Row.

Punit, A.E , Profils of Poverty in India, B.R. Publishing Corporation, Delhi (1982).

Rao, B S., and Deshpande, U.N. Poverty: An Interdisciplinary Approach; Somaiya Publications (1982).

Rao, V.K.R V., An Essay on India's National Income. George Allen and Unwin Ltd., London, 1938.

Rao, V.K.R.V., Food Nutrition and Poverty in India. Vikas Publishing House, 1982.

Rountree, B S., Poverty—A Study of Town Life; Macmillan, London, 1922.

Sarma, P.P., Dimensions of Rural Poverty. Daya Publishing House, Delhi (1987).

Sen, A.K., Choice of Technique, Oxford University Press, 1962.

Sen, A.K., On Economic Inequality. Oxford University Press, 1973.

Sen, A., Poverty and Famines: An Essay On Entitlement and Deprivation. Oxford University Press, New Delhi (1982).

Sinha, R., Pearson, Peter, Kadekodi, Gopal and Groyory, Marry. Income Distribution Growth and Basic needs In India, Vikas Publishing House, New Delhi, 1979.

Srinivasan, T.N., and Bardhan, P.K, (Ed.). Poverty and Income Distribution in India. Statistical Publishing Society, Calcutta, 1974.

Thimmiah, G., Inequality and Poverty. Himalaya Publishing House, Bombay, 1985.

Townsend, P. (ed.). The Concept of Poverty. Heinemann, London, 1970.

Wedderburn, Dorothy (ed.). Poverty, Inequality and Class Structure. Cambridge University, Press, 1974.

Journals :

Adiseshiah, M.S., "Poverty: its what, why and how". Yojana, Vol. 32, Nos. 1 & 2, Jan., 1988.

Ahluwalia, M.S., "Rural Poverty and Agricultural Performance in India". The Journal of Development Studies, April, 1978.

Atkinson, A.B , "On the Measurement of Inequality" Journal of Economic Theory, Vol. 2, 1970.

Balakrishna, S., "Incidence of Rural Poverty in Recent Years. Behavioural Sciences and Economic Development, Hyderabad, Vol. 3, No. 1, January, 1971.

Bardhan, P.K., "On the Minimum Level of Living and the Rural Poor. A further Note Indian Economic Review, April, 1971.

Bhatty, I.Z.. Inequality and Poverty in Rural India. In Sankhya Series, C. Vol. 36, 1974.

Bhaya, H.. "Growth and Justice—an understanding of the nature of our poverty. Yojana, Vol. 32, Nos. 1 & 2, January, 1988.

Burney, S.M.H., "Community Involvement must for raising living standards". Yojana, Vol. 32, Nos. 1 & 2, Jan. 88.

Chaudhary, K., "Socio-Cultural Dimension of Poverty. Yojana, Vol, 32, Nos. 1 & 2, January, 1988.

Dalton, M., "The Measurement of the Inequality of Incomes", Economic Journal, Vol. 30, 1920.

Dandekar, V.M., and Rath, N., "Poverty in India". Economic and Political Weekly, Vol. VI, Nos. 1 & 2, 1971.

Dandekar, V.M., and Rath, N., "On Measurement of Poverty, Economic and Political Weekly, Vol. XVI. No. 30 (1981).

Dandekar, V.M., "On Measurement of Undernutrition. Economic and Political Weekly, Vol. XVII, No. 6 (1982).

Dangwala, M.L., "A Profile of Poverty and Unemployment in 12 villages". Indian Journal of Agricultural Economics, Vol. 33, No. 2, April-June, 1975.

Daswani, C.J., "Poverty of Commitment" Yojana, Vol. 32, Nos. 1 & 2, January, 1988.

Datta, B., "Diagnosis of Destitution. Yojana, Vol. 32, Nos. 1 & 2, January, 1988.

Desai, S.S.M., "Poverty in India—The Magnitude of the Problem". The Economic Times, Vol. VII, No, 245, Friday, Nov. 28, 1980.

Dogra, Bharat, "Poverty—Challenge Response and Some Question. Yojana, Vol. 32, Nos 1 & 2, 7an., 1988.

Dutta, B., "On the Measurement of Rural Poverty in Rural India". Indian Economic Review, Vol. 13, No. 1, 1978.

Gupta, S.P., and Datta, K.L., "Poverty Calculation in the Sixth Plan" Economic and Political Weekly, Vol. XIX, No. 15, 1984.

Jayaswal, R., "Our Greatest Asset—the People". Yojana, Vol. 32, Nos. 1 & 2, January, 1988.

Krishna, Raj, "Income, Proverty and Unemployment. Economic Times, May 15, 1980.

Krishnaji, N, "On Measuring and Incidence of Undernutriton". A Note on Sukhatmes Procedure". Economic and Political Weekly, Vol. XVI, No. 22, 1981.

Krishnaji, N., On Measuring Incidence of Undernutrition, what is a consumer Unit, Economic and Political Weekly, Vol. XVI, No. 37, 1981.

Lakdawala, D.T., "Growth Unemployment and Poverty". The Indian Journal of Labour Economics, Vol. 21, Nos. 1 & 2 April-July, 1978.

Madalgi, S.S., "Hunger in Rural India 1960-61 to 1964-65. Economic and Political Weekly, Annual Number, Jan., 1968.

Madalgi, S.S., "Poverty in India—A Comment. Economic and political Weekly, Feb. 20, 1971.

Minhas, B S., "Rural Poverty, Land Redistribution and Development Strategy, Facts and Policy". Indian Economic Review, Vol. 5, 1970.

Ojha, P.D., and Bhatt, V.V., "Pattern of Income Distribution in India, 1953-54 to 1956-57". Reserve Bank of India, Bulletin, Volletin, Vol. 17, 1963.

Ojha, P.D., "A Configuration of Indian Poverty : Inequalily and Levels of Living" Reserve Bank of India Bulletin, Jan., 1970.

Prasad, Kamta, "Poverty Alleviation—Issues and Options". Yojana, Vol. 32, Nos. 1 & 2, January, 198९.

Rajaraman, Indira, "Poverty, Inequality and Economic Growth; Rural Punjab 1960-61 to 1970-71. Journal of Development Studies, Vol. 2, No. 4, July, 1975.

Rao, V.K.R.V., "Some Nutritional Puzzles. A Note". Economic and Political Weekly, Vol. XVI, Nos. 28 & 29, 1981.

Rao, V K R V., "Measurement of Poverty, A Note". Economic and Political Weekly, Vol. XVI, No. 35, 1981.

Sathe, Vasant, "Refusal to think; an act of cowardice". Yojana, Vol. 32, Nos. 1 & 2, January, 1988.

Seetharam, G.N., Transformation through Technology. Yojana, Vol. 32, Nos. 1 & 2, January, 1988.

Sen, A.K., "Poverty, Inequality and Unemployment. Some Conceptual Issues in Measurement" Economic and Political Weekly, August, 1973.

Sen, A.K., "Poverty, Inequality and Unemployment. Economic and Political Weekly, Special Number, 1973.

Srivastava, P.N. Educate People to Eradicate Poverty, Yojana, Vol. 32, Nos. 1 & 2, January, 1977.

Stewart, Frances and Streetan, Paul, "New Strategies for Development; Poverty Income Distribution and Growth", Oxford Economic Papers, Vol. 28, No. 3, 1976.

Sukhatme, P.V., (1977), "Measurement of Poverty based on Nutritional needs Bulletin of the International Statistical Institute, Vol. XLVII—Book, 4, Contributed papers.

Sukhatme, P.V. (1978), Assessment of Adequacy of Diets at different income levels". Economic and Political Weekly Special Number, August, 1978.

Sukhatma, P.V., "Measuring the Incidence of Undernutrition—A Comment". Economic and Political Weekly, Vol. XVI, No. 23, 1981.

Sukhatme, P.V., "On Measurement of Poverty". Economic and Political Weekly, Vol. XVI, Nos. 32, 1981.

Suryanarayana and Iyengar, "On Growth and Equity in Indian Planning During 1961-62 to 1973-74". The Indian Economic Journal, Vol. 33, No. 4, April-June, 1986.

Suryanarayana and Iyengar, "Poverty Indicators", Economic and Political Weekly, Vol. XIX, Nos. 22 and 23, 1984.

Thon Dominique, "A Poverty Measure", The Indian Economic Journal, Vol. 30, April-June, Nov., 1983.

Visaria, Pravin, "Poverty and Unemployment in India". Indian Journal of Agricultural Economics, Vol. 35, No. 3, July-September, 1980.